POETRY
OF
LOVE,
LIFE
AND
LOSS

This edition published 2019 by

The Lime Press

POETRY

OF LOVE,

LIFE

AND LOSS

*"The greatest pleasure of writing is not what
it's about, but the music the words make."*
Truman Capote

BY
BARRIE PURNELL

ACKNOWLEDGEMENTS

Thanks to all those people, lovers, friends and
enemies, who have helped to shape my life
and so provided the inspiration for
the poetry in this book.

Thanks to the poetic songwriters of the sixties,
who I have always envied, and members of
the Retford Writers Group for their
knowledge and encouragement.

Special thanks to Patricia Bryn-Jones for all of her
help in assembling this anthology, and guiding
me through the untold mysteries of
punctuation and the digital age.

CONTENTS

LOVE Page No

LIFE   Page No

LOSS   Page No

Dedicated to all those who need poetry when they are in love, sad or just mad at life ...

And to Rosemary

LOVE

A MILLION MILES FROM LOVE

"Some people live just looking for someone to die for."
Dominic Riccitello

She came at me from nowhere
Arriving silently like mist,
Something about her chilled me
But it seemed futile to resist.
She said," I've travelled far to reach you,
I have been following the dove,
I've come a hundred miles past heartbreak
But I'm a million miles from love."

She was a penitential pilgrim,
From love's betrayal in retreat,
Seeking love and affirmation
To reverse her previous defeat.
She sought the safety of my arms
Her lips demanding to be kissed,
You could see that she had suffered
From the marks upon her wrists.

Her face was a mask of innocence,
Though she was danger in disguise,
Her little black dress was drooping,
Like the circles beneath her eyes.
Eyes that were full and glistening wet,
With a thousand unshed tears,
Because all the love she needed
Was buried deep beneath her fears.

In her search for love and happiness
There was no room for compromise,
But even when she was laughing
There was a sadness in her eyes.
She was carrying a burden,
Just what it was I didn't ask,
Yet always knew she was listening to
Those heartbeats from her past.

She was like some pretty songbird
That fools you as she flies,
Singing you some simple song
That covers up all her lies.
She spoke truth only in her silence,
She survived on the love she stole,
Spilling words like kisses from lips
Which could suck out your soul.

Although I saw her body naked,
I could never lay bare her mind,
She locked the door to her secrets
With a key I could not find.
She had too many other lovers
Already hidden inside her heart,
I was just another bit part actor
She needed to play a part.

She was acting out a tragedy
In which I was to play the fool,
A game that I could never win
Because she made all the rules.
She was drowning in her history
She was too far from the shore,
Bleeding love from a thousand wounds
Inflicted on her from before.

It seems there is no limit
To the pain a lover can endure,
I could only share her suffering
I could not supply the cure.
She was searching for a saviour,
Guided by angels from above,
She's one hundred miles past heartbreak
And still a million miles from love.

AN ILLICIT AFFAIR

"What of soul was left I wonder when the kissing had to stop?"
Robert Browning

Bedroom Boredom
Forbidden Fruit
Casual Chatter
Flirtatious Flattery
Amorous Advances
Furtive Fumbling
Passionate Petting
Copious Copulation
Sexual Satisfaction

But then

Developing Disillusion
Carnal Comparisons
Jaundiced Jealousy
Carping Criticism
Angry Accusations
Bitter Battles
Predictable Parting
Retrospective Regrets
Solitary Sadness

Just another typical illicit love affair.

RESSURECTION

"How can I begin anything new with all of yesterday in me?"
Leonard Cohen

When I fell in love with her beauty
We were young, naive and free,
So close there was nothing between us,
I was her and she became me.
It was for her that I had been waiting,
It was for her that my body yearned,
But she told me she gave away nothing,
Any favours would have to be earned.

She quickly overcame my defences,
She had developed love to an art,
Before I knew it she had me surrounded
And had slipped past the guards to my heart.
She carried me away, with her dancing,
To a place where I'd never been,
She transported me with her love songs,
To places that I'd never seen.

Expecting nothing from all our devotions,
Caring not for who it was on the cross,
We weren't looking out for a saviour,
To the priest we were already lost.
We were drowning in oceans of kisses,
Bathing in lakes of freshly shed tears,
The smell of her skin stupefied me,
Her arms held on tight to my fears.

I surfed on the waves of her ardour,
I was helpless, she gave me no choice,
She beguiled me and hypnotised me,
With the tilt of her nose and the lilt in her voice.
We thought we'd be together forever,
But at the bank of love our balance was low,
We had to refund all the passion we'd stolen,
We knew you have to pay the debts that you owe.

Real life intruded into our passion,
There were decisions which had to be made,
We'd exhausted our credit with Eros,
The piper now had to be paid.
She said she'd become a jet setting model
On the catwalks of Rome and Berlin,
And I'd become some sort of chemist
Making the drugs that kept models thin.

Our affair never overcame separation,
Our passion soon cooled and was spent,
Addresses were lost, or forgotten,
The promised letters never were sent.
We lost touch and found other lovers
Then, by chance, our paths crossed again,
It was at a charity event that I saw her,
Surrounded by urbane looking men.

I wondered if she would remember,
Or act as if we'd never met,
I'd be hurt if she had forgotten,
Was I that easy for her to forget ?
I slid into the sphere of her vision,
Did she find fortune and fame ?
With relief I saw her smile at me,
It was a sad smile just the same.

We talked of our past infatuation,
And the journeys we'd taken since then,
We were now both different people,
That was a love we would never regain.
We breathed the same air at that moment
But we were no longer as one,
Even when her arms were around me,
The closeness we had once was gone.

When I saw that the party was ending
I couldn't let that be the end of the line,
I offered to deputise for her taxi,
To be with her for just one last time.
She lived in a posh part of Cheshire,
At number six Montgomery Drive,
As we approached I could see that the houses
Were designed to impress those who arrive.

I stopped at her gates and, turning to me,
She said, "I'll e-mail you sometime next week,
We'll arrange to have lunch together,"
Her lips brushed a kiss on my cheek.
I knew that this wouldn't happen,
Our worlds had moved too far apart,
I could see that, despite her affection,
There was no room for me in her heart.

She may not have become a model,
But lived the lifestyle just as well,
Sashaying up her catwalk of a driveway
In her little black dress by Chanel.
I watched her disappear through the doorway,
I hoped she'd turn round for my pride,
But she went in without glancing backward,
The gates closed with me still outside.

Did she steal a look out of the window ?
In my mind I'll pretend that she did,
But in my mind I knew it was over,
In love's gamble, I had been outbid.
I pushed her into the recess of remembrance,
Where she'd lived for decades before,
Her ghost had been finally banished,
I didn't need her love in my life anymore.

But I hope sometimes she thinks of me fondly,
Of promises made when we were young,
And when she's lonely, and searching for someone,
It will be my name on the tip of her tongue.
She'll never know just how much I missed her,
How she hid in my heart all this time,
How I remembered the way that she loved me,
Because she will never be reading this rhyme.

Your first love may always be special
But remember, looking back is always the same,
You only remember the good times
Forgetting all of the hurt and the pain.
To avoid rejection and disappointment,
Just remember your first love with affection,
Don't try breathing life into dead lovers,
You will very rarely achieve resurrection.

IF YOU TAKE LOVE AS YOUR MISTRESS

"Somewhere between love and hate lies confusion,
misunderstanding and desperate hope."
Shannon L. Alder

Some things in life you can't comprehend or control,
Affairs of the heart and that which lies deep in your soul.
Love is a mistress you cannot command or constrain,
An enigma, a mystery, you can never explain.

If you are looking for love then you had better beware,
If you take love as your mistress, she isn't forgiving or fair.
She will mess with your mind until nothing is what it seems,
She is too dreamy for real life and too real for dreams.

A fallen angel, who comes to you while you sleep,
Searching your mind for commitments to steal and to keep.
You are in a prison without bars and her hypnotic hand
Will hold you, without touching, wherever you stand.

She will bind you tightly with jealousy and with mistrust,
Ambushing you with a confusion of passion and lust.
When all your emotions are laid out naked before her,
She'll clothe them in your tears, which is all she can offer.

If you take love as your mistress she will seduce you with lies,
If she succeeds you'll find she's taken your soul as her prize.
She can be all things to all men, enslaving you with her charms,
As you lie naive and unguarded in some lover's arms.

She is without mercy, demanding surrender right from the start,
Leaving you defenseless against another attack on your heart.
Picking love as your mistress is just a gamble you take,
It's your heart you are risking, if you lose it will break.

The book of love gives you the odds, if you bother to read,
Why, when so many have failed, are you so sure you'll succeed ?
Love's a one way journey with no route map or chart,
Few successfully end it from the many hopefuls who start.

If you're lucky she'll give you eyes that won't shed any tears,
And a transfusion of trust to banish all doubts and fears.
She will weave you dreams from roses to blot out yesterday,
You'll have no regrets, and be happy, that she stood in your way.

She'll invade every part of you, from your head to your heel,
Mere words on a page can't describe how she'll make you feel.
She'll ignore all your weaknesses telling you that you're strong,
Giving you romance known before only in poetry and song.

So go ahead and take love as your mistress, that is if you dare,
Remember my warning, from someone who's already been there.
Only take love as your mistress if you can handle the role,
She may be your one true love and you've nothing to lose …

But your soul.

THE SCRAPBOOK OF MY MIND

"I don't want to repeat my innocence. I want the pleasure of losing it again."
F. Scott Fitzgerald

I think back to the first time I saw her,
Blond hair and cherry red lips,
Looking out from her cosmetic counter,
Pencil skirt hugging close to her hips.
She didn't realise she was a beauty,
Her pose belied her age of seventeen,
The stiletto heels threw her hips forward
Like the pictures in Vogue magazine.
These images are easy to recall,
And are very well defined,
They are always with me,
Safely pasted into the pages of the scrapbook of my mind.

I saw her grow into a young woman,
Walking with me arm in arm,
In her Mary Quant skinny rib sweater
And her perfume by Paco Rabanne.
She was confident in her beauty,
Poised and self-possessed,
But our affair drifted to destruction
On the backs of uninvited guests.
I see her clearly after all these years,
Her images are easy ones to find,
They are always with me,
Safely pasted into the pages of the scrapbook of my mind

We met again at the funeral of a friend,
After more than forty years had passed,
Her beauty was still there to see
The pale blue eyes still flashed.
A few more lines around the eyes,
When I made her smile,
And still that sensual, hip-swaying strut,
The clothes still worn with style.
The fresh faced innocence of youth
Had been left far behind,
But I still have those early images,
Safely pasted into the pages of the scrapbook of my mind.

I wonder if she too has a scrapbook,
That she hides inside her mind,
In which she pasted in my picture
From when our lives were intertwined ?
When she's feeling lonely,
And she's drowning in the blues,
Does she turn the pages of her book
To find that person she once knew ?
Will a wistful smile form on her lips,
From the remembered love she'll find,
In those half-forgotten images,
Safely hidden inside the pages of the scrapbook of her mind ?

IMAGES

"Memories, even bittersweet ones, are better than nothing."
-Jennifer Armentrout

In the colour of the autumn leaves
I see your clear brown eyes,
I see you in that soft spring breeze
That swirled the skirt around your thighs.

In the ice white, kiss soft snow,
I see your peach downed skin.
In the textured glass of a window,
I see the dimple in your chin.

I see you in the sweet spring rose,
Which even bears your name,
Its fragrance lingers where it grows,
Like your perfume by Guerlain.

I see you in the ocean waves
That roll in to break upon the shore,
Then when I close my eyes to dream
I see your image even more.

I see you in the morning sunshine,
Light filtering through your hair,
In every shadow I see your outline,
But when I reach out you're not there.

In the stillness of a southern night
I hear the whispers from your heart,
Reminding me what I always knew,
That you were our loves greater part.

You left me partway through the show,
Yet your face won't leave my mind,
When you left me, how was I to know
You'd leave all these images behind ?

FINGERPRINTS

"Don't know if I saw you I would kiss you or kill you." Bob Dylan

It was a strong addictive drug, the love we had discovered,
A preordained relationship where everything seemed right,
Wrapped in our infatuation, desiring nothing but each-other,
Writing wordless poems with our bodies in the night.

No words found on any printed manuscript,
Can describe a love from which all modesty is stripped.

I am left to wonder how it ever came to this,
The warmth of summer chilled by the damp autumn of truth,
You christening my pillow with salt tears,
Me, a sad spectator to the funeral of my youth.

I could have filled the largest book on any library shelf
If I had printed all your lies, and those I told myself.

Where did it go, that unquestioning devotion ?
Two dreamers driving unmapped highways in the sky,
Our routes drifting apart, almost unnoticed,
Both of us too self-obsessed to ask each other why.

The manner of your leaving was a traitor's masterclass,
All you left was a lipstick imprint on your empty glass.

Why did you share with me all your most secret secrets ?
When you embraced me did you just pretend ?
When did you steal from me everything I'd ever lost ?
Why did you say you loved me and you were my friend ?

When I pressed you for answers you refused to meet,
You just printed one hundred 'sorrys' on an A4 paper sheet.

Now I look at you from the other side of loneliness,
Clothed in the rags of regret and remorse,
Trying not to reach back into yesterday's gloom,
Where hides the pleasure of love and the pain of divorce.

But on my body and my heart, your fingerprints remain,
As a reminder of the dangers should I fall in love again.

ARE ALL LOVERS SINNERS ?

"There is a charm about the forbidden that makes
it unspeakably desirable."   Mark Twain

I could hear the distant music
From a thousand violins,
Playing out a requiem
For a million lovers sins.

Then a choir of angels
Started singing sweet and low,
To the multitude of lovers
Around the crosses down below.

A sweet, sweet voice spoke to them
Asking all of those to leave,
Who had ever been unfaithful
Or had attempted to deceive.

Everyone began to leave,
Walking away from the light,
Taking their immorality
Back into the safety of the night.

The choir was singing a sad song
For those lovers who were lost,
For the souls of their companions
And the hearts that had been crossed.

Where have all the lovers gone
Who are trustworthy and true,
Who are fit to join the angel choir,
Could it be me… or is it you ?

No one who loves can be perfect,
No one in love can be wise,
In the dark rooms of a lover's heart
You'll find a library full of lies.

Are we doomed to join those sinners
Who will go down in the flood,
For breaking all our lovers' vows
That were sanctified in blood ?

Will we too hear the distant music
From those thousand violins,
To inform us of our failures,
To remind us that we've sinned ?

THE TRUTH ABOUT LOVE

"Love is the most beautiful of dreams and
the worst of nightmares."   *Aman Jassal*

My lover did not moralise or preach,
She did not lecture me, theorise or teach,
Saying there was nothing to be frightened of.
        She said she would tell me the truth about love.

My lover won the battle for my heart,
She said her love would not be à la carte,
She was more bird of prey than turtle dove.
        Only she told me the truth about love.

My lover told me there was no equality,
No place for subservience or modesty
In the love that she was thinking of.
        Only she told me the truth about love.

My lover wrote to me of betrayals overheard,
And the inevitable debts these had incurred,
All of which she had noted and made records of.
        Only she told me the truth about love.

Dylan, Cohen, Bowie, and Young,
Provided the background music to our lives.
My lover said love is a delusion for which we strive,
An affliction and a torment to survive,
And not the sweet love they were singing of.
   Only she told me the truth about love.

No one could help when my lover broke my heart
When she told me that it was time for us to part,
Or tell me why I had walked with her so far,
Why only a lover knows who you really are,
Why a lover's wounds leave a soul deep scar,
Although inflicted with a velvet glove.
   Now I know the real truth about love.

If your search for truth has been in vain,
And you're looking for a reason for your pain,
You will find love's truths are only spoken
By lovers whose hearts are already broken,
Destroyed from inside by loves raw emotion,
Who've kissed lips a thousand lies have made use of,
   Only then will you know the real truth about love.

I HAVE WRITTEN YOU A POEM

"Poetry spills from the cracks of a broken heart,
but flows from one which is loved."
Christopher Paul Rubero

I have written you a poem,
So you will always remember,
Just how much I have loved you
Since you took my surrender.
My heart is in the meter
My soul is in the rhyme,
Reminding you all that matters
Is you, and me, and time.

My words tell you of a love
Stripped of familiarities disguise,
Frail fragments of the truth
Plucked from a labyrinth of lies.
If you ever find the lines
Of our love becoming blurred,
My poetry will be the key
To unlock the truth in my words.

On leaving I meant to say I love you,
But we just kissed instead,
Those abandoned words now lodging,
Like malign judges in my head.
I miss your easy laughter,
The taste of the salt in your tears,
Your words of love on leaving,
I take to keep as souvenirs.

The words that pass my lips
Never reveal just how I'm feeling,
That's why I wrote these lines
While you were quietly sleeping.
Words to heal our scars,
To make our broken love whole,
The words are an ocean joining
The distant shores of our souls.

I'll try and remember to tell you
I love you, as often as I can,
If sometimes I don't it's because
I am a just a mediocre man.
There may be times when I don't see
The hurt behind your eyes,
Or the sadness in your smile,
When I have to say goodbye.

When I fail, just take out my poetry
And read the words out loud,
They will remind you of the sunshine
And push away the clouds.
Wrap my words around your heart,
Let them sit softly on your lips,
Driving any doubts and fears
Out of your toes and fingertips.

My words are written so in part
I will always be with you,
They lay bare my soul,
Imperfect, but the best I can do.
Every word is a kiss from my lips,
And an embrace from my arms,
Every line is a rampart
Built to defend you from harm.

Every verse is an army to defeat
All your doubts and suspicions,
My love inextricably woven
Into its composition.
Whenever you read it,
No matter where you happen to be,
It will enfold you in all
The love that binds you to me.

MEANINGLESS LETTERS

"There is a time for departure, even when there's no certain place to go."
Tennessee Williams

You were older, experienced,
I was saying goodbye to youth,
In that long gone summer,
I couldn't have loved you more.
I can still see you clearly,
With your tied back, dyed black hair,
Stood at the edge of the tide,
Silhouetted against the moon blanched shore.

A glance from you enclosed me,
I gave little thought to the
Brittleness of your beauty,
Or the elasticity of your truth,
Which brought about my humiliation.
The ardour of those love drowned days,
Was soon quenched by the
Damp numbness of cohabitation.

Everyone knew those reasons
You gave for returning late,
Were fabrications of lies that
You found so easy to create.
I knew only the lies I told myself,
Mistaking dreams for truth.
Maybe that was just a measure
Of my innocence and youth.

My questions fell like raindrops
Into the sea of your silence.
You painted permanent tears
Upon my face, yet felt no guilt.
When you finally deserted me,
For another lover, I was naively hurt
That you had so easily discarded
The love that we had built.

So it is, when I hear your new
Lover too has been found wanting,
I feel no satisfaction, just surprise
At the meagerness of my emotion.
I hear you've sent me letters of reconciliation,
Reminding me that your first letters were
Love laden missiles, aimed at my heart,
Their passion needing no translation.

.

Your face is now lost in the flood
Of remembrance, an image decayed,
When once it was a private screen
On which my life was played.
I have no desire past love to redefine,
Neither am I wanting retribution.
Our affair is just yesterday's trivia
Relentlessly diminished by time.

I draw the curtains from my watery eyes
And turn towards another day.
The twilight world outside is still
Painted in monochrome grey.
Mist writhes into the corners of the morning,
A cold light falls through the window.
Two orphan sparrows huddle close on the sill,
Echoes of your broken promises fade into the new day.

I do not crave your kisses,
I am not longing for your return,
You left me staring at lost yesterdays,
Your goodbye hurt me like a burn.
Sometimes in the mirror I think I see a familiar reflection,
With relief I realise it is just the ghost of your rejection.
Where your picture hung is now just a darker patch on the wall,
And your meaningless letters now litter the hall.

OBSESSION

"Freedom begins on the other side of obsession."
Marty Rubin

We met on a chill day in November
I was hungry, forlorn and frightened.
She offered me shelter and comfort,
The burden I carried was lightened.

She said, "Come I can offer you refuge
I have an antidote here for your pain,
I will turn the light off on your nightmares,
I won't ask you to confess or explain."

I was happy to take up her offer,
She possessed the flawless beauty of youth,
If I had looked behind that pretty face,
I may have cracked the code to her truth.

She offered me some liquid refreshment,
She told me to just drink it all up,
I didn't know the drink that she offered,
Was infatuation in a cracked plastic cup.

I drank deeply and felt myself falling,
The cup slipped from my hand to the floor,
The smile evaporated from her lips as she said,
"We won't need that cup anymore."

"You'll be my partner descending to darkness,
For all my offenses, you'll pick up the bill."
I said that I couldn't, I said that I wouldn't,
She said "Sorry, but you must and you will."

I should have run, I should have departed,
For some reason I didn't make that choice,
An invisible web seemed to hold me,
Spun round me by the lies in her voice.

I had drunk from her cup of obsession,
I had given my freewill to her,
I became the foodstuff for her hunger,
I'd pay for any debts she'd incur.

She said, "You must sign your surrender,
Put all your inhibitions aside,
You abandoned yourself freely to me,
You did it with your eyes open wide."

But she had mistaken need for desire,
My eyes too blinded by tears to see,
She wanted not love but possession,
She wasn't my saviour but my enemy.

She had invaded my whole being,
My mind now had a mind of its own,
Her mind a mystery kept well hidden,
Behind the disguises you were shown.

She let no one inside her defenses,
Never forgiving, always up for the fight,
Her guard always up, never lowered,
No one really knew her but the night.

Her ears were deaf to my protests,
Her eyes those from which tears never shed,
Her heart was like ice, only colder,
I love you, words her lips never said.

Having no moral compass to guide her,
Never driven to repay any debt,
Giving no one her heart's secret password,
She never experienced pain or regret.

A terrorist disguised in a black lacey dress,
Switchblade held in a black velvet glove,
Holding me to ransom for a million tears,
Stealing my heart but killing off love.

Why wouldn't she give me my freedom ?
Why did she write everything down ?
Why was she always so close beside me ?
Why were my arms always so tightly bound ?

I was trapped by her burning obsession,
I was desperate to leave and be free,
Whether you're in a refuge or a prison
May be only a matter of degree.

I asked my friends if they would help me,
They said they couldn't afford the time,
I asked for help from the law who said,
Obsessive love was not yet a crime.

I asked my doctor could he prescribe a cure
For the sickness I was speaking of,
He looked in every one of his healing books,
But he could find not one cure for love.

Then I turned to my God for an answer,
I asked the priest to take my confession,
Appealed for a way out of my prison,
He said there is no way out of obsession.

To love is one of God's prime commandments,
Obsession's just love by some other name,
You know love is God's gift to all lovers,
If you leave her, God will know who to blame.

I was trapped and I could see no way out,
I walked down to the bridge at the river,
She had consumed all of me that mattered,
There was nothing else I could give her.

I felt a soft tap on my shoulder,
It was a lover from some previous time,
She opened the door to my deliverance,
Told me the decision would have to be mine.

I told my tormentor I'd be leaving forever,
Not to follow, as there would be no reward,
Her passion had exceeded my allowance,
Her love I could no longer afford.

I could not afford all the suffering,
I couldn't afford to live in her shrine,
I couldn't afford all of her maintenance,
I just couldn't afford to give her my time.

I left quickly without looking backwards,
Into my saviour's enfolding, forgiving arms,
She didn't question me or pass judgement,
She didn't moralise or quote me from psalms.

Maybe she didn't have all of the passion,
Or have the perfect beauty of youth,
But she had the honesty of experience,
And the matchless beauty of truth.

JUST A LITTLE BIT

"Remember not the sins and offenses of my youth."
Book of Common Prayer

Please don't think ill of me now I'm gone.
Try to remember all the good times,
All the funny and misunderstood times.
Don't list down everything I did wrong,
That list would then be much too long.

You want me to pay for my indiscretion,
And, although I alone carry the shame,
Remember that you too were to blame.
Maybe even if you can't forgive my transgression,
You'll find a little bit of love still in your possession.

If you put me on trial, I would have to confess
I have no excuses, I have no more to say,
I didn't value our love and it just slipped away.
You must hate me now with all the hate you possess,
But could you just try to hate me a little bit less.

I know there is no jury that would ever acquit,
If they heard of all my lies of former days,
And all of my cheating and deceitful ways.
If you don't love me now, I know I'd deserve it,
But maybe you could still love me, just a little bit.

Even our saviour forgave people their sins
Can you not show the same compassion ?
Betrayal could be the price we pay for passion,
Who knows where the betrayal first begins ?
Love's not always played to the sound of violins.

You know I never wanted our love to end,
So if we meet by chance in some cold town,
And a little bit of your love could still be found,
Take pity on me please and just pretend,
Hold me like I was still your lover, not just a friend.

THE PROBLEM WITH WORDS

"Be careful with your words. Once they are said,
they can be only forgiven, not forgotten." Anon.

I met her in the long hot summer of sixty three,
On a surfing beach in south-western France,
I wanted to grab her attention with my poetry,
I just hoped it would give me a chance.

The words I needed were all there in my head
But were cryptically concealed in my mind.
They were words I'd heard or words I'd read,
But those damn words were so hard to find.

Like drunks my words staggered and fell off the line,
Forming a jumbled lexicon piled at my feet,
My pen itself appeared hostile and malign,
Leaving me staring at a sterile white sheet.

Too late, I found the words I wanted to say,
Another troubadour had captured her heart,
My love turned to malice, when I heard her say,
That I was not in the race from the start.

So in place of verses full of love and desire,
The words were those of resentment and spite,
I ignored her contrition and appeal for ceasefire,
Because I was fully absorbed in the fight.

I dealt out my words like sharp stainless blades,
Each syllable a barbed arrow of pain,
Each sentence simply one more heartbreak repaid
For that love lost down in Aquitaine.

It was so much easier to find words for my malice,
Fired like bullets from a gun to the page,
My jealousy a willing accomplice
To my humiliation, frustration and rage.

Too late, I realised the words that you write
Can fatally wound without leaving a trace,
Each word is forever and lies there in plain sight,
You can't recall them or have them replaced.

I wish I hadn't wasted my words on anger,
But then what is life without any regret,
For a poet each word they write is a failure,
There are so many failures I need to forget.

If you are trying to win yourself a new lover
Don't try ensnaring her with eloquence and rhyme,
When you find her, tell her simply that you love her,
Using poetry could be just a waste of your time.

ALL SHE WANTED WAS MY TIME

"Little things I should have said and done,
I just never took the time."   Wayne Carson

When each year seemed forever,
And I was young, as I recall,
Nothing was beyond my reach,
I thought I had it all.
All my silver and all my gold,
That emerald egg by Fabergé,
If I could do it all again, for her I'd give it all away.

Just one of Casanova's congregation,
Scavenging for love others let fall,
Pretending I was still in the game
But knowing I had lost it all.
Alone I lie here waiting for
The darkness that will fall,
If I could love her just one more time, she could have it all.

If I could do it all again
There would be no more lies,
No more insincere goodbyes.
I would kiss her lips more sweetly,
Love her more completely.
It was she who had the need,
I could not see beyond my greed.
With so many lovers still to find
The register remained unsigned.

Back then our love was newly born,
Now the wedding dress is torn.
I squandered far too many years,
I was the cause of far too many tears.
I had my chance, I chose to hide.
Now it's too late to turn the tide.

Now I'm getting near the end,
Close enough to hear him call,
Look at the beggar I've become
When I could have had it all.

Inside my world of pain
Her love is all I know,
If I could do it all again,
I would have never let her go.

When she came to me in sorrow
I offered her everything that was mine,
She said she never coveted my riches,
All she had wanted was my time.

LOVE'S NEVER EASY

"A man who rejects you is simply clearing the way for the one you deserve."   Naide Obiang

It wasn't the happy ending
That she was always dreaming of,
She may have lost you as a lover
But she hasn't yet lost love.

Just because she may be hurting now
Don't think she'll turn the other cheek,
She won't be overwhelmed by misery
Just because you never speak.

She doesn't need you for her passion,
She doesn't need to worship at your throne,
She doesn't need your body close to her,
She can make it on her own.

She needed the pain of your rejection,
So she could more easily recognise,
When real love finally comes along
And puts the stars back in her eyes.

You gave her less than she was worth,
You have no claim to any of her tears,
You will not even be in her memory
Looking back from future years.

Some day she may find your address
And wonder just who you were,
Or see you with some other lover
And just be glad that it's not her.

She came to me to cure her hurt,
To take away all of her pain,
I gave her my shoulder to cry on
Until she falls in love again.

She doesn't know that I love her,
Maybe I've known her for too long,
I feel I'm living a lover's tragedy
Like in a Leonard Cohen song.

Her pain is inflicted by her lovers,
Which she endures time after time,
My pain is just to watch her suffer
And know her love is never mine.

Love's not there to make you happy,
It's not there to make you feel secure,
It's there to make you suffer
And see how much pain you can endure.

GOING BACK

"And now the final frame, love is a losing game."
Amy Winehouse

I am going back from whence I came,
To where everything has stayed the same,
I am going back to where I was before we met.
I am going to make a planned retreat,
Back to all those old familiar streets,
They will hide me and help me to forget.

I am going back to where the shore
Is marked by the sea's withdrawing roar,
Where the hills hold the horizon in so near,
Where the church bell will call me in
For the priest to forgive me when I sin,
Where I am surrounded by all that I hold dear.

I am going to steal your hidden key
So that I can set my spirit free,
Leave behind all your lies and your deceit.
I'll wait for the dying of the light,
Leave in the blackness of the night,
I won't be there to taste the tears of your defeat.

I am going to leave my burden here,
I am going to try and disappear,
I will leave all our history behind.
I will make sure I cannot be traced,
I will have my records all replaced,
And they will dig me a grave you'll never find.

I've had too much sorrow, too much pain,
To try and love you once again,
I am returning to where I was before,
Before you loved me and destroyed me,
Before you wounded and adored me,
I don't have the heart to love you anymore.

I am going back to where it all began,
Back to where this child became a man,
To that place that I thought I had outgrown.
In time all the wounds you left will heal,
My memories will all return to real,
I am going back to the place that I call home.

THE WAR IS OVER

"So the great affair is over but whoever would have guessed
it would leave us all so vacant and so deeply unimpressed."

Leonard Cohen

When I told you our affair was over you reacted with surprise.
I honestly believed by now, that even you would realise,
Your deceptions and betrayals I no longer can forgive,
Our love a desert of duplicity, somewhere I couldn't live.

You don't need me for a citadel, where you can run and hide,
When the next ephemeral lover casts your love, and you, aside.
I don't want to argue with you, discuss it with you, or explain,
Our affair was simply something neither of us could sustain.

Why do you ask if you can return to live with me again,
Knowing that would result in yet more misery and pain ?
Our love proved at best to be a weak and transient spark,
Sufficient only to illuminate one small corner of the dark.

We were just two random rocks, both hewn by chance,
From life's inexhaustible quarries of uneasy circumstance.
You promised exclusivity but the contract was never signed,
You loved me with your body but never with your mind.

This is not the time to regret it, resurrect it, or to weep,
We both made many promises too difficult to keep.
I opened up my heart to you but you still demanded more,
A rip tide dragging me away from the safety of the shore.

You knew I could not swim yet pulled me out into the deep,
You were an insurgent in my head driving out my sleep.
I asked you for a cease fire between my love and yours,
You demanded my surrender but couldn't get my signature.

I lie alone on my barren bed staring blankly at the moon,
Which throws your absent shadow across the empty room.
You're there hiding, like an uninvited guest, inside my brain,
Your pleas for forgiveness haunt me like an unwanted refrain.

If a cure for one more broken heart is what you're talking of,
I can offer you my sympathy but I cannot give you love.
Thinking of all the feuds we had and realizing, but too late,
How fragile is the border fence between true love and hate.

So don't tell me you're surprised that our affair didn't last,
Our dreams are just worn out yesterdays, fading to the past.
Your deceit left us talking through a veil of poisonous pretense,
My failures just ammunition for you to use in your defence.

Now you will reap the harvest of the lies that you have sown,
Believe me, you don't need me, you will manage on your own.
You were only ever an itinerant gypsy girl visiting my bed,
Now at last our war is over and not a drop of blood was shed

HOUSE OF REFLECTION

"There is one art of which people should be masters — the art of reflection."
Samuel Taylor Coleridge

There is a house set by the River Idle,
Where willows bow their branches to cry,
Their tears lost in the river's dark waters,
Mirror your confusion as you pass by.
The house holds very tight to its secrets,
You went there hoping you would find
Forgiveness for your indiscretions,
Not for me, for your own peace of mind.

In the hallway musicians are playing
In the Viennese romantic tradition,
Dream loaded couples dance around them
Chasing rhythms in counterfeit competition.
You looked around for a partner to join them,
They were dancing with love as the prize,
When you found the trophy already taken
Tears rolled like pearls from your eyes.

The fires are tended by disgraced vestal virgins,
Their once bright halos are tarnished and dim,
Their flesh, as white as pure alabaster,
Disfigured by the purple veins of their sin.
For a fee they will provide you with service,
You tried to unburden yourself of the blame,
Though they listened and gave you their comfort,
When you left them, you still felt the shame.

In a room where windows are curtained,
Poets gather in the gloom of the day,
To write about all the love and the passion
That has never been stood in their way.
On the walls they have recorded their failures,
And all the sins for which they must atone,
You read and recognize your own anguish,
They have shown you that you're not alone.

A pale light filters through the Rose Window
On a priest accepting penitential confessions,
From lovers renewing their original vows and
Seeking forgiveness for previous transgressions.
All that you ever gave to me were promises,
From lips now swollen and heavy with lies,
You spoke of a love that would be forever,
Then whispered a hundred goodbyes.

Next door the unshaded light bulb
Throws stark shadows on the clinic white wall,
Of entwined bodies on the bed in the corner,
But you can see no sign of love there at all.
Did you reflect on your own betrayal ?
Was passion without love worth the price ?
Did it satisfy your need for belonging ?
Was it worth all that you've sacrificed ?

When you go out into the transparent morning,
Knowing your past owns you, there is no retreat,
You use your silence to wrap round your sadness,
Regret follows as you walk down the street.
I too regret our love ended in failure,
We realised in love you can't have it all,
You chose to share your love with another,
 I chose failure rather than taking the fall.

FALSE ALARM

"The open-hearted many, the broken-hearted few."
Leonard Cohen

Flying south on a thundery night
Into Cannes.
She sat beside me in her cherry red suit
By Balmain.

Lightning struck, she grabbed my arm
Squeezing it tight.
Then I realised it wasn't desire,
Simply fright.

False alarm.

Maybe falling in love has become
An addiction,
Will I ever find love, or is true love
A mere fiction ?

Misunderstandings, of those
I've had plenty.
I wonder, will my whole life
Just turn out to be,

One long false alarm ?

YOU CAN'T BUY A CURE

"What is hell? I maintain that it is the suffering of being unable to love." — Fyodor Dostoevsky,

I make my way down a lonely barren street,
A rising sun stretches shadows up the walls,
Vacant eyes stare from grimy cafe windows,
And somewhere a lonely hound-dog calls.
In a cheerless café I stopped to ask,
If there was a hotel on the road ahead,
One man turned his face from the window
And, in a troubled voice, he said,
"Many people have passed by
On their way there but I never learned,
If any of them ever did reach it,
Because I never saw any return."

Finding the hotel I spoke to a girl at the desk,
She had the look of a faded rock 'n roll star,
I said I'd heard they could cure heartbreak
She didn't speak, just rang a bell on the bar.
A young woman stepped out of the shadows
Saying, "Your journey is now at an end,
I can give you your fill of passion
But for true love you'll have to pretend.
I can heal your heartbreak,
If you just let me take control,
And all I ask from you as payment,
Is just a small part of your soul."

"I will take you beyond the limit of longing,
Beyond the heartbreak that you feel,
But you must give yourself completely
If your heart I am going to heal."
I yielded, she gifted me her passion,
I left all lovelorn thoughts behind,
But she loved only in flesh and blood,
I never occupied her mind.
Her emotions had been choked off
By heartbreak's tourniquet.
She made a smash and grab raid on my soul,
Saying, "Now is the time to pay."

With a sad smile she showed me to the door,
And said "I've taken what you owe,
You will suffer no more heartbreaks
But now it's time for you to go."
I asked her, why do I feel this way ?
She answered with a wistful smile,
"Your life is now one without passion
To which you must be reconciled.
You were told the price that you would pay,
To which you so foolishly agreed,
What we took from your soul was love,
Which you thought you didn't need."

"You will never again feel the passion
Of a heady love affair,
Or the loneliness of losing a lover,
Or the pain of love's despair."
She had kept her side of the bargain,
No more loneliness for me,
I could not give, or feel, another's love
But from heartbreak, I'd be free.
If you are betrayed by a lover,
Don't take a journey like mine,
You can't buy a cure for a broken heart,
It will only be made better by time.

IRONY

"The greed to be loved is a fearful thing." C.S. Lewis

They say opposites attract
So we should have been alright.
You loved the dark, I loved the light.
You loved parties, I loved bed,
You loved Poldark, I loved Father Ted.

You loved the heat, I loved the cold,
You loved the new, I loved the old.
You loved the sun, I loved the snow,
You loved the TV, I loved the radio.

But we were both self-centred and
Loved ourselves much more than
Anything else.

Ironic, isn't it, that the only
Thing we had in common was
The one thing that destroyed us.

THE END OF A LOVE AFFAIR

For Rosi 1974 - 2015

We met by chance, it was a brief encounter just one night,
We talked and laughed and kissed goodbye and said we'd write,
Words to be lost in the darkness and not examined in the light.
Then her letter told me of her love, in words so erudite,
They broke through my defences and set my soul alight.
From that chance encounter a lifetime love affair took flight.

Stealing time for days together, nights we couldn't say goodbye,
We hid inside each other's hearts, oblivious to passers-by.
I told her I'd always make her happy and never make her cry,
I would give her everything I had and never ask her why,
That from all previous lovers my bonds I would untie,
And all my secret places, I would let her occupy.

She soon knew all about me, understood everything I said,
She had the key to thoughts I kept locked up in my head.
Dylan's words the soundtrack to our lives when newly wed
She played me Cohen's songs as we lay together in our bed.
Living in the moment, no thought of what might lie ahead,
We pushed away reality wrapping ourselves in youth instead.

Our love was all embracing, it was a selfish love I know,
No time for family or friends or that nightly TV show.
Pursuing our ambitions, we watched our fortunes grow,
Searching for that croc of gold at the end of life's rainbow.
As years passed ambitions faded, but how were we to know
We had found what we'd dreamed of that long, long time ago.

We had all of those possessions once looked at from afar,
A house with an indoor swimming pool and a silk lined boudoir,
The chairs they were by Chippendale, with a walnut escritoire.
On the wall a painting by Rossetti, we purchased in Dunbar,
The gold and silver jewellery was from an Istanbul bazaar,
And outside in the garage, a big black Bentley car.

When I lost my love, dreams dissolved in the cold October rain,
Her photographs, and my memories, are now all that remain
To remind me of those sunnier times, that I never can regain.
I was left feeling like an addict who's deprived of his cocaine,
All those sympathetic words raised tears I struggled to contain,
Just realising that my life would never be the same again.

If life could only stay the same but that's never going to be,
Time's thief steals love from everyone, this time his victim's me.
The pain of loneliness or death is just a matter of degree,
The night ignores my cries for help, it is my enemy,
A dark crevasse down which I fall where no one hears my plea,
Only when we masquerade as lovers in my dreams am I set free.

There are no words for my despair at losing her for good,
Does it matter now I loved her and did everything I could ?
If to bring her back, I shout her name into the graveyard wood,
Just an echo of my voice returns, like I always knew it would.
We rarely see him coming, the reaper with his scythe and hood,
And if we did, would he have cared about our grief, would he
have understood ?

Immortality is not for us, we are just nature's slave,
A random hand selecting who's next for the grave,
However many deeds of kindness done or sinners we forgave,
However many penances we take to the Cardinals' conclave.
I cannot stop the tears of sadness for a love I could not save,
I promised my love many things, but never promised to be brave.

I now look enviously at young lovers, like a secretive voyeur,
Time, once a thief of love, is now a devious saboteur,
Distorting all my images of love so they all fade and blur.
My love was not so brief that I can forget how we once were,
Yet, as if by accident, in the future I know a day will occur
When I'll not think of her even once,

And this is the last line I will write her.

LIFE

MY SECRET LIFE
Retford Writers Group 2015

In real life I am conventional, I wear a suit and tie,
A middle class professional is who I typify.

In real life I am a scientist, an engineer by trade,
I fix things when they're broken, I know how they are made.

In real life I am God fearing, no one knows I've sinned,
I don't annoy my neighbours, my lawns are neatly trimmed.

In real life I avoid an argument, I am both mild and meek,
I do not like impetuosity, I think before I speak.

In real life my pension is why I worked hard all my life,
I achieved a certain status, I had a well-respected wife.

In my real life my friends are all very similar to me,
But now I've got to thinking if that is how it has to be.

———————

In my secret life I am a rebel not wanting to conform,
I want to be a writer who can inspire and can inform.

In my secret life I am a romantic seeking out the truth,
Making up for all those years I wasted in my youth.

In my secret life I'm Cohen, writing a memorable song,
Composing lyrics like Bob Dylan righting every wrong.

In my secret life my songs are lovers aphrodisiac of choice,
The bereaved use my poetry to give their grief a voice.

In my secret life my words will make broken hearts whole,
Serving to illuminate long forgotten corners of the soul.

But all these flights of fancy, I always had assumed,
Would stay inside my secret book inside a darkened room,
In real life when I joined a group of other aspiring writers,
The light inside my darkened room became a little brighter.
I started writing poetry, although admittedly traditional,
It reflects my life, misspelt, crossed out but essentially original.
It took many years for my writing to begin, but in my defence,
I have found in real life it is best when poetry lags experience.

FREE VERSE

*"Free verse is not a new metre any more than sleeping in a
ditch is a new school of architecture."   G.K. Chesterton*

They said to me forsake your simple rhymes
Free verse is what describes a poet best,
Those arbiters of taste, those powerful men,
The editors who publish Poetry Today.
That which reminds them of childhood nursery rhymes
Is no longer a measure of a poet's worth.
Look more to the poems of Walt Whitman who,
Using assonance and alliteration,
Ensures his verse flows smoothly from the tongue.
But we know the poetry remembered best,
By those of us who enjoy, rather than judge,
Is that where rhyme implants it in our brain.
We all recall verses by the likes of
Hardy, Shelley, Browning or John Betjeman,
Are they, and all their kind, damned as mere rhymesters,
Because some words tend towards a single sound ?
While Wordsworth's Daffodils is oft on someone's tongue,
His unrhymed Prelude comes less readily to mind.
Yet I cannot escape the need to understand
The secret of writing in this free verse form.
Maybe I could use some sort of subterfuge,
And intertwine a rhyme within each line,
So satisfying my urge to versify.
But this would simply be a fool's deceit
To disguise my inability to use
That hidden art which gives free verse its form.

They say my verse must have no set length of line,
No rhymes and no set rhythm too.
I am told beware the iambic pentameter,
Unless your verse is to be blanc.
So I ask, what can I use to drive my words
To the bottom of my still empty page ?
They say follow the rhythm of your normal speech,
And listen to the sounds made by your words,
That is when your free verse poetry will come.
This must be the most difficult of tasks for
Those of us taught to live life within the rules.
Experience tells me no rules lead to chaos,
Which is anathema to the ordered mind.
That must be the secret of this free verse construction,
To bring order out of chaos with no set rules.
If no rules exist then how am I to judge,
If any of the lines I have written here
Amount to poetry, in free verse form,
Or just the scribblings of a bored old hand ?
All the while those damn rhymes form and drip
From the corners of my mouth onto the page,
Searching for a line they can complete.
There is no place for them in my free verse,
They drift away homeless outcasts on my breath.
What is this, more advice you give me now ?
You say it doesn't really matter anyhow !
No, please don't tell me after all this time,
You liked it better when I made it rhyme !!

LIFE IN THE CITY

."I have never found salvation in nature. I love cities above all."
Michelangelo

Take me away from the city,
Away from the noise, the dirt, the heat,
To the tranquility of the countryside
Far away from those hard city streets.
Away from the jostling crowds,
With their fixed faces devoid of smiles,
Acting as if with one purpose,
But all with their own particular style.

Away from those claustrophobic canyons
Of concrete and bronze reflective glass,
I want to stop walking on paving slabs
And sink my steps in the grass.
I don't want to see rows of brownstone buildings
Through the morning chill,
I need to look out to a big sky horizon,
And see the far off, blue hazed hills.

Take me away from the city,
From the cars and buses and trams,
From the inevitable frustrations
Of interminable traffic jams.
Away from the fumes and the litter,
Away from the dirt and pollution,
And those six day sinners, who on Sunday,
Go to church to seek absolution.

Let me escape metropolitan madness
And the pretentious coffee shop crowd,
I need an instant injection of nature,
And to shout my frustration out loud.
I want to get away from the loneliness
That the city crowds can bring,
I want to be in the life of my neighbour,
I want to be where I can hear birds sing.

Take me out into the country,
Beneath the skies in which skylarks soar,
So I can walk across dew spangled grass
Where no footsteps have been before.
A silence made louder by soft spring rain
That scours sunlight from the sky,
With the sweet smell of the wet earth
Enfolding me, like a soft sung lullaby.

I want to hear the sound of the bells,
Ebbing and flowing on the tide of the wind,
From the church, where the priest in his cassock,
Prays for redemption for those who have sinned.
Let me breathe in the air from the hillside,
And hear the sound of an invisible stream,
I want to be outside the city lights,
See stars glitter where the sun has just been.

I want to walk down that secret lane,
Between head high hawthorne hedges,
Past the ruined farmhouse on the corner,
Where swifts' nests cling onto the ledges.
To the wood where the badgers and foxes,
Are defended by an army of trees,
All their trunks standing up to attention,
Their green heads all bowed down by the breeze.

They appear to reach down to touch me,
Their rustling leaves calling my name,
Telling me, if I don't leave the city now,
I will have only myself to blame.
But I think I will stay in the city,
Despite the dirt, the noise and the heat,
I would miss too much the excitement,
And the tramp of a thousand feet.

IN DEFENCE OF TRADITION

"Modernism despairs of human history and abandons the idea of a linear historical development." Georg Lukacs

I am a human by birth but a poet by choice,
My poetry gives this artist's abstraction a voice.
When I write of the beauty of stars in the sky,
Or the pain in the heart born of saying goodbye,
They condemn my use of rhyme and repetition,
On the slippery foundation of perfidious opinion.
They say that I'm guilty, but do they have proof ?
I only ever tried to write down the truth.

I have spent many hours searching for beauty,
As a poet, I was surely just doing my duty.
You disciples of Ginsberg, you lovers of Pound,
You have contempt for the past and for lyrical sound.
You are literature zealots, who seek to destroy,
All those past compositions that many others enjoy.
You blame me for exposing your pride and pretense,
My words are my weapons, they are my only defence.

You put me on trial, but failed to get a conviction,
My sonnets were outside your court's jurisdiction.
You asked was I guilty ? You asked did I transgress
Against your perceived wisdom ? My answer was yes.
You keepers of disrupted syntax and experimentation,
You killers of rhyme, you lovers of prose fragmentation,
You wrote me a confession which you asked me to sign,
Because I valued the truth, I was forced to decline.

You don't like my words, yet even ideologues see,
The fact I can write them is what it means to be free.
I think you're pretentious, you think my work is absurd,
But I've only ever tried to cast a tune down in words,
Trying to find hidden ideas that my mind has caught,
Releasing them from impenetrable thickets of thought.
Maybe I could be wrong and you may prove to be right,
That I've been ensnared by the very words that I write.

You say my poetry is obsolete, observing outmoded rules,
But I write for believers, not for proselyte fools.
You subvert my intentions, punctuating all of my lines,
With meaningless phrases, as revenge for my crimes.
You've confiscated my sonnets, you are shredding them fast,
In your desperation to break all links with the past.
All of our previous beliefs you've overturned,
Disregarding all the earlier rules that we've learned.

We yearn for the poetry of Longfellow and Poe,
All those lyrical poems penned a long time ago.
You crucified romantic tradition on a Modernist cross,
Burying Coleridge, the Mariner and the Albatross.
We're now emerging from your self-serving, sententious gloom,
We have rolled that boulder away from the tomb.
With brains, that are hardwired to rhyme and repetition,
Lyrical poetry is written to enhance the human condition.

It survives in the remembered verses of a million songs,
Your work lies in vaults beyond recall, where it belongs.
I now write in secret my sonnets and verses,
That you say are traditional and therefore subversive.
You thought you had won but we were never defeated,
Those lines now rewritten which you had deleted.
Conforming non-conformists, loving your own reflection,
Our army is now growing through your disciples' defection.

I have started a petition, I've got ten thousand names,
Very soon other poets will join in our campaign.
So now in the back rooms of backstreet cafes we lurk,
Still fighting the war against all your modernist work.
My disciples are gathering, they meet in the night,
They will soon be re-armed and ready to fight.
To fight for that poetry that sings to your soul,
Replacing all those rhythms and rhymes you modernists stole.

I have gone underground, I am biding my time,
Waiting for the poetry elite to return to order and rhyme.

TOMORROW

"By what right do I, who have wasted this day,
make claims on tomorrow?" Alain-Fournier

Night flows in to surround the house,
Turning the view from the window
Into my reflection.
In a sky, filled with pin bright stars,
A solitary cloud kisses
The cheek of the full moon.
Skeletal branches of birch trees,
Scatter light from the street lamps,
Which flicker like Christmas decorations.

Two cats have claimed the floor
Beneath the radiators, one on her back,
Paws stretched up towards the heat,
The other laid out like a tiger skin rug.
Their relaxed attitudes do little
To drag me out of my state of
Late night lethargy.

I have been trying to write,
As yet unsuccessfully.
I am not searching for perfection,
Tonight mediocrity would do.
Scattered papers, contaminated
By unfinished poems, lie helpless
On the indifferent table top.

I haven't embraced the discipline of patience,
My hand moving across the paper,
Like a panic-stricken general, trying to
Outmanoeuvre the chaos of my thoughts.
A jumble of incoherent phrases
Tumble onto my expectant papers.
I give up for the night.

An ever optimistic calendar
Stares at me from the wall,
Telling me there are sufficient tomorrows
For me to complete at least one
Of these malevolent poems.
But it's getting late.
I will do it tomorrow.

Yes tomorrow,
I will do it tomorrow.

IF I WAS AS OLD THEN

"One doesn't recognize the really important moments in one's life until it's too late."   *Agatha Christie*

Recalling my youth as I get old,
I've realised how arbitrary life is,
How I wasted many opportunities,
Following superiors who controlled,
The ideas and theories I was taught,
Not getting the answers which I sought,
Not realizing life would be so short.
I wish now that I had been more bold,
And ignored the false truths I was told.

Now I have time to pause and reflect,
On advice received when in my youth,
A time when I was searching for the truth,
When I gave too much unearned respect
To teachers, whose honesty I didn't doubt,
Not questioning what they talked about,
Not knowing what to take, or leave out,
Leaving me unprepared, in retrospect,
Which of life's chances to take and which reject.

They say the young must be controlled
But what then is youth, if not the time,
To find your role within life's pantomime ?
It's a time to take your chances and be bold.

A time when, with the arrogance of youth,
You have no doubt it's you who know the truth,
Just believing, not seeking any proof.
You know, without requiring to be told,
That soon enough it's you who will be old.

If only I was as old then, as I am now,
How much easier life would have been,
Knowing everything I have done and seen,
Not having to ask my masters, when and how ?
Yes, if in my youth, I had today's experience
To treat my elders with less reverence,
Thinking more rebellion than obedience,
I would have furrowed many a senior's brow,
If I had been as old then as I am now.

When asked by youths for my advice,
On how to navigate a path through life,
Avoiding too much agony and strife,
I tell them, trust yourself to throw the dice.
Don't trust vain people, who will let you down,
Ignore false prophets, whose views abound,
Trust yourself to know where truth is found.
Know in life, only you will pay the price,
Only you can find the way to paradise.

AGE

"Wisdom is the reward for surviving our own stupidity."
Brian Rathbone

When I was young I was immortal, the whole world was mine,
The future, a blank canvas on which dreams could be defined.
I ran laughing through storms, raindrops sparkling on my jeans,
The sun was hot, winds were warm, when I was in my teens.
New paths were there to walk along, when I was young.

Life was easy, school an annoying interlude between holidays,
Lifelong friendships forming before going our separate ways.
My first love affair was with Patsy, I carved her name into a tree,
The village beauty, it felt so good when she danced with me.
There were love songs to be sung, when I was young.

It was the fifties, rock and roll, the emergence of the teens,
A drape coat and crepe soled shoes, hair styled with Brilliantine.
Riding my Triumph down country lanes, risking life and limb,
A leather jacketed, Gene Vincent look alike, wishing I was him.
Beat poets were on my tongue, when I was young.

Listening to all those protest songs, about race, power and war,
Full of idealistic notions of how they'd got it wrong before.
In my naivety I thought we could change the world at large,
Not realising we could never reach the faceless men in charge.
Tears were shed, hands were wrung, when I was young.

Student life was carefree, just parties interrupted by exams,
While trying to understand thermodynamics' baffling diagrams.
This was a time for love and dreams, it was youths' curtain call,
Ambition yet to show its face inside our cloistered college hall.
Life was just so much fun, when I was young.

Now I'm old my future is uncertain, my time left has decreased,
Dreams now of past adventures, personal inertia has increased.
Now the sun's too hot, and accentuates the retreat of my hair,
Storms only get me wet and snow is just another cross to bear.
I'm always much too hot, or much too cold, now I am old.

Time is passing more quickly than it did when I was young,
Those lifelong friendships ending with requiems being sung.
I see my empty house, into which my whole life is now distilled.
And recall my dreams, now all destined to remain unfulfilled.
I remember all those principles I sold, now I am old.

I return to the village of my youth, Patsy's name still on the tree,
But, try as I might, I can't recall her face which saddens me.
The canvas my dreams were painted on now in shades of grey,
When young I never thought I'd be as old as I am today.
That's how it is, I'm told, when you are old.

With age has come perspective on the idealism of my youth,
Replaced by scepticism of beliefs peddled to me as truth.
I realise power and money come out winners in life's game,
And, looking back in history, I see it has always been the same.
I see world problems just get retold, now I am old.

Now I can reflect on all the things I have said and done,
All the battles that I have lost, all the races that I have won,
All those greasy career ladders I tried so very hard to climb,
Are of no consequence at all, when viewed through the
telescope of time.
I have few more of life's pages to unfold, now I am old.

St. MICHAEL the ARCHANGEL

A.G.W. Pugin described the spire of this church as 'a poem in stone'.

It

Sits back

From the road,

As if not wanting

To impose itself on

The denizens of Retford,

Who pay it scant attention as

They pass, except when the sound

Of a sorrowful funeral bell, draws their

Gaze briefly upward to the silhouetted tower.

Built by the rough hands of many artisan masons,
Who had an unfounded confidence in the future,
A mature structure that stands uneasily against
Its adolescent, secular neighbours. A thirteenth
Century monument to faith wearing its angularity
Like a skin. Dedicated to the archangel, wrongly
Called a saint, it stands held tightly against the
Incline, confining the River Idle's waters far below.
The small graveyard, which nestles in its lea, is
Permanently shadowed from the sun, the dead
Walled in, as if to stop them from witnessing the
Unholy life outside. We know nothing of their
Lives, they were quietly forgotten in their death.

Perspiring fat bottomed mothers haul protesting children
Up the hill, and sharp suited young executives hurry
Downwards towards their amber liquid lunch.
They are uncaring and indifferent to this
Ancient sanctuary's history. That is left
To a diminishing band of disciples,
Who go on Sundays, to affirm
Their faith, and cling in
Hope to the almost
Empty pews.

WILL THEY HEAR YOU ?

"Beware that you do not lose the substance by grasping at the shadow."
Aesop

In the center of the city,
In amongst the rushing people,
No one has the time for talking,
No one sees although they're looking.
They don't see the Georgian buildings,
Or the stained glass in the windows,
These are just objects on their journey
To be glanced at and forgotten.
Like the beggar in the doorway,
No one cares that he is hungry,
Or that he is cold and lonely.
They are hurrying home to dinner
Thinking of what's on the table,
They can smell it, taste the wine,
They can't stop, don't have the time.

Look at all the vacant faces,
Eyes cast down to mobile phones,
Studying unwanted e-mails,
Posting tweets and Facebook photos,
Texting friends of the minutia
Of their tiresome dreary lives.
But there are some who catch your eye.
A young man in a grey serge suit,
Laptop clutched so tightly to him,

A trendy man in washed blue jeans
Contemplating his fading youth.
An Arab girl in brown Hijab
Shutting out the evil city,
Girls in fifties vintage clothing
Found on Cancer Campaign Counters.
A blond with full Rossetti lips,
Unknowingly Pre-Raphaelite.
You will never get to know them,
Who they are or where they live,
For in an instant they are gone
Each one going their separate way.

Once again you are alone,
Alone with all of your ambition,
Which took you to the top position,
Fruits of your private tuition.
At the top but isolated,
Lonely though the crowds surround you.
Is this the way to spend your life,
Love cast aside for your career,
Befriending those you don't respect
With weasel words you will regret,
Whilst friends are lost through choices made,
Links broken by benign neglect ?

All you faceless city people
In your quest for fame and fortune,
Beware life passes by so fast,
When you reach your destination
You may find it's all illusion.

All those business life decisions,
That gave you all those sleepless nights,
You'll find were not real life at all,
No, not real life but just a game,
And to win you sacrificed
The love of family and friends,
In pursuit of financial gain.
Now if in your despair, you call
For help from those who were your friends,
You may find they have no time
For someone they knew way back when.
Do not listen to those siren sounds,
That tempt you to the city lights,
Like moths, you're likely to get burned
And fall unnoticed to the ground.
Beware you may have just become
That beggar freezing on the street,
With everybody passing by,
Too busy with their self-deceit,
To hear you calling to be saved.
You're just another lonely voice,
One of thousands who are seeking,
Reassurance and forgiveness,
From those who they have wronged before.
Just ask yourself, from where you stand,
Can you still see where your friends are,
And do you think, that if you need them,
Anyone will hear you calling ?

DOWN DEEP

"I opened the doors to Hell and walked in gleefully."
Liz Thebart

You took me down to a place that was deeper than deep,
To a place that had never seen light,
Down to a place that was darker than dark,
Darker than the blackest of nights.

You took me down to a place where love's never been,
Where the days have said goodbye to the sun,
Where your life depends on the malevolent hand
Of a dealer who can't be outrun.

You took me down to a place that was deep in despair,
Where the streets ran wet with our tears,
A place where you plan to go just for an hour,
Then find you are trapped there for years.

I was deeper than I had ever wanted to go,
I was deep down, I was lonely and lost,
Everyone there was searching for something,
Nothing we found was ever worth what it cost.

I wanted your love, that's why I followed you down,
Where penalties for failure were severe,
Where the Candy Man had my skull picked clean,
With no hope that I would ever go clear.

You took me deep down into the entrails of life,
Surfing that snow white wave for kicks,
Living in the middle of a red eyed delusion,
From that syringe with it's dream-loaded fix.

You took me down to a place that was deeper than deep,
You said going deep would shut out my pain,
And you somehow disguised pain as pleasure,
By divorcing my thoughts from my brain.

No matter how I tried I couldn't break free,
I had lost the game, now I was paying the bill,
Alone in the dark, without love, without hope,
Down so deep you can find me there still.

LOOKING INTO THE FIRE

"Fire is a powerful thing. It cleanses as it destroys." Patricia Briggs

When I look in the fire, I see flickering traces
Of forgotten faces and faraway places.
But who is it I see ? Is it an enemy
Seeking indemnity for previous duplicity ?
Or buried family
Reminding me ?

When I look in the fire, I see the Second World War.
Did Dresden settle the score for what went before ?
The London blitz, Coventry, Auschwitz ?
Victory it will assist, the air marshal insists,
Do you think God acquits
All hypocrites ?

When I look in the fire, I see Hiroshima in flames.
Did they feel any shame ? Who was to blame ?
Killers flew high in the Japanese sky,
Did they ask why ? Did they cry ?
As thousands die.
American Samurai.

When I look in the fire, I see Joan of Arc at the stake.
She fought for Christ's sake, which was her mistake.
Her battle was won in the town of Orleans,
But she was undone by the Bishop Cauchon.
Burnt in Rouen,
Only nineteen years gone.

When I look in the fire, I see Guy Fawkes funeral pyre,
The bell tolls in the spire as the flames go higher.
Gunpowder plot was mooted, Guy Fawkes was recruited,
Catholics persecuted, thirteen executed,
Bonfires instituted,
Fireworks distributed.

When I look in the fire, I see a million suns.
Born when there were none, now dying one by one.
Making me think of infinity, the Holy Trinity,
Of earth's fragility, the laws of relativity.
Sun's nuclear activity,
Sustaining humanity.

When I look in the fire, I see an image of hell.
Will I be able to tell, when I say my farewell,
Am I on Satan's list for being atheist ?
Or as a humanist, will I just cease to exist ?
Or by angels be kissed ?
Will I be missed ?

IF ONLY THEY KNEW

"Truth sits on the lips of dying men."   Mathew Arnold

Take time to look inside yourself, but only if you dare.
Alone in the anonymous darkness of the night,
Are you ashamed of what you find hidden there ?
From childhood, we learn the art of flattery and deceit,
To ease our progress through this life
Where truth is held hostage to our conceit.

If only people could see those thoughts stored in my head,
All the insincerities and all the lies,
That lay behind the platitudes I said.
The expressions of sorrow and crocodile tears that flowed
For another's hurt and tribulation,
To me it was just another debt I owed.

How many acts of betrayal have I hidden in my mind ?
How many Judas kisses have I bestowed
On sweethearts when love had made them blind ?
People see my lips smiling but not the sadness that's inside,
I'm concerned my tears will betray me,
Dissolving that mask behind which I hide.

We spend most of our lives trying not to give offence,
Surviving on the false flattery of friends,
Living a life we know is one glorious pretense.
No one really knows me, only the version I project,
You too are mostly hidden, like an iceberg,
You tell me only what you want to, that's all I can expect.

I stand beside you, I only really know your name,
I only see your reflection, your disguise,
I do not see your hypocrisy and shame.
Have you added up the lies ? Have you done the sums ?
To see where you'll be, on the scale of honesty,
On that day when the final reckoning comes.

Maybe when I am dying I will drop the veil at last,
And just for those last few precious moments
Will be my true self, shorn of the pretense of the past.
It is too late now, too late for me to start again,
I will just have to live this lie and hope
I'm not exposed by one who's better at the game.

RENEWAL

"We change, we are change, trying to hold on to any of it is futile."
Debbie Lynn

The pale light diffuses through the clouded window
Signaling the start of yet another new day,
Not just an ordinary day, but the first day of spring.
The morning's irritations fade when I look out to see
The world shining fresh and new after the rain.
New life is returning after winter's vandalism.

Pussy Willow catkins show like tiny fingers.
A few carmine red shoots are already visible
On the pruned rose stems, prompting a memory of
The breathtaking blooms of last summer's display.
They are leading actors in nature's endless resurrection,
Now their stems stand stark against the dark, damp earth.

The rising sun throws dancing shadows of leaves
Across the ivy clad, railway sleeper wall.
The broader shadows of clouds glide across the path.
A pale, lemon yellow, primrose pushes through
Its winter ravaged, worn out rosette of leaves,
And lifts a pretty head towards the tepid sun.

Raindrops, like pearl drop earrings, hang from branches
Under which scattered troupes of febrile insects dance.
An insolent noisy robin challenges every intruder,
While a tiny, ever mistrusting, wren retreats
Into the safety of it's hidden, priest hole home.
Somewhere in the windless morning a blackbird sings.

Vibrant saffron yellow cups of crocuses
Are painted onto the lawn's bright green canvas,
Moss occupies spaces between the sandstone slabs.
The fresh green shoots of the Iris give little
Indication of their future azure beauty,
The exclamation marks of the flower world.

I love the spring, when everything looks brand new,
But I feel sadness too that it is so ephemeral.
So are our lives within eternity,
We can't hold on to beauty, it is bound to fade.
We should enjoy our springtime while it lasts,
All too soon it's over and autumn leaves cover the ground.

I am reaping the harvest of all the deeds I've sown,
Both kind and hurtful have had their consequence.
Unlike flowers that fade, returning good as new each spring,
There is no rebirth for this creature I have grown.
My finality is assured by inescapable decay,
I envy the innocence of the reborn flowers.

The springtime of my years is now long since gone,
I give no thought to all those dog-eared yesterdays,
Remembering little of my spring, except its beauty.
I am living through the dying of my life,
No flowers will grieve for me when I am gone,
They will bloom again to please a stranger's eyes.

IN LIFE'S WINTER

"Everybody cries and everybody hurts, sometimes."   R.E.M.

When your life enters a winter spell
It can be difficult to face,
You feel alone and isolated
In a bleak and hostile place.
A place where only pain and hurt
Are available on demand,
Where the people all around you
Don't appear to understand.

Bitter winds send withered leaves
Whirling around your feet,
No moon lights your way down
The dreary endless street.
Jack Frost sets an ambush for you
In the icy cobbled yard,
You are just one more reluctant actor
In life's cruel charade.

The clouds are weeping tears
For your summertime's demise,
The leafless trees forlorn and downcast
In their winter guise.
An avalanche of sorrow flows
From winter's cruel mouth,
The spectral grey sky decorated
By the last geese flying south.

Condensation on the window pane
Does its best to hide,
The white crests of the breakers,
On the wind whipped sea outside.
The sound of surf is masked
By the moaning of the wind,
Like the gods are punishing you,
It's as if they know you've sinned.

.

The bitterness of winter is just
The price you have to pay,
For the taste of summer berries
And the roses' sweet bouquet.
Desolate days stretch before you,
You must just wait for them to end,
Surviving on the memories
Of summer days with friends.

Life's winter reminds us that
We cannot choose our season,
There is no point in us mere mortals
Trying to fathom out the reason.
Despite your belief that no deity
Has control of your affairs,
You kneel before a Buddha
And tease some other god with prayers.

Mortality is all we've got,
That's why I'm hanging on hard to you,
You say dreams are your reality,
Pain the only thing that's true.
You think you've lost control of everything,
But you still own the way you feel,
Morphine may steal your hurt,
But not our love, you know is real.

I say I know how you're feeling,
But your pain cuts through my bluff,
I'm trying to love you better
But know it's still not good enough.
I long to set an ambush for your agony
And cure you with one tender touch,
Please don't make me feel a stranger
Because I'm loving you too much.

Look to the sun, which always wins
It's battle with the suffocating night,
You're not asking anyone for pity,
Just freedom, from pain's relentless bite.
You see the spring sunshine reflecting
Off of the languorous morning tide,
And know that, however hard your winter,
You and beauty have survived.

Do not despair, believe, there is still time,
Your race is not yet run,
Fix your eyes on the eastern horizon,
You'll be the first to see the sun.
Your heart will beat away the pain,
Your spirit will win the final war,
We'll have time to walk again, like lovers,
Between the ocean and the shore.

LIFE CHOICES

"Aging is an extraordinary process where you become the person you always should have been."　　　*David Bowie*

I met a man I could not see
But there he was in front of me.
I met a man I could not feel
But he was there and very real.
I am your life, the stranger said,
I am everything you've ever seen or read,
I am every thought you've ever freed,
I am your every evil, unkind deed.

I am all the beauty you have created,
Everything you have ever loved or hated.
I am every card you have ever dealt,
All the love you have ever felt.
I'm here to tell you, up to this date,
You've chosen too little love, and too much hate,
Too little generosity, too much greed,
There is too much hurt you've left unhealed.

I am giving you a chance to change,
And your priorities to rearrange.
Few get this chance I'm giving you,
Their own life to look at and review.
Normally I'd wait until you're about to die
Before I flashed before your eyes.
I won't be appearing to you again,
But I'll still be there, inside your brain.

If the opportunity should arise someday,
For you to meet your life, what would it say ?
Would the scales come down on the side of good,
Or are you unsure if they would ?
It made me think about the life I'd spent,
One of selfish discontent.
I could have given more and taken less,
Not sacrificed others for my success.

If I changed now, was it too late
For me to put my record straight,
Before the appointment that I made,
With my life when at death's barricade ?
At the end, when they discuss my reputation,
Will it be a eulogy or an assassination ?
I chose to change but only time will tell,
If I will sing in heaven or burn in hell.

THE UPRISING

"In later times my idols fell, for I learned that they were only men."
Bob Dylan

Politicians ask for our views then try to defy us.
That pinstriped executive army all try to deny us.
Promising future riches, thinking they can buy us.
They think we are naïve,
But we are no longer deceived,
They'd understand the anger in what we say
If they lived like us for just one day.

The Bishops with their sceptres, purple robes and finery
Stand in great cathedrals preaching to us of life's mystery,
Using incense to cover the stench of their own hypocrisy.
They tell us our sins to forsake,
To surrender our wealth for others sake.
We may accept their sanctions, for rules transgressed,
When they give their own riches to the dispossessed.

Lawyers who profit from other people's distress,
Talk in labyrinthine riddles, benighted clients to impress,
Money, not morality, is how they measure their success.
But we have seen through their game,
Now it's our turn to claim.
When we expose their crimes to everyone,
They'll be judged for all the wrongs they've done.

Experts who manipulate statistics to fit the theory of the day,

None are independent, but compromised by those who pay,

Their reputation for infallibility is in irretrievable decay.

The rules of the game are reset,

Their certitude they will regret.

They used to tell us why and how

But, sat at our computers, we are all experts now.

These people think they're superior due to an accident of birth,

They have no perspective of what freedom is really worth.

They thought they would fall heir to all the riches of this earth,

But they had not included in their plan,

The uprising of the common man.

The time has come to bring about their ultimate defeat,

That ruling, privileged minority, the liberal elite.

THE WIDOWER

"Each age is a dream that is dying or one that is coming to birth."
Arthur O'Shaughnessy

He is an old man.
Age has freckled his hands and arms,
His face marked and weathered like an old wall.
He sits alone, in the curtained gloom,
Surrounded by the odds and ends of someone else's life.
He is resisting, but his childhood is relentlessly closing in.

He is bent double like an old beggar,
Just managing to raise a tired smile,
As the scent of summer flowers invades the window.
He's become used to death leaning over his shoulder,
Time has proved a traitor to his early promise,
And is now his only scarce commodity.

He is bound around by boredom,
An armchair setting the limits of his global horizon,
Memories now distorted by the cruel lens of time.
His old friends have left him,
The beauty of life now lies only in his mind,
Aching joints now his sole constant companion.

.

The winter rain knocks on the roof
Of the two up, two down stone built cottage,
Which he had fallen in love with at first sight.
It is now looking old and worn like him,
And past subsidence has left it leaning slightly,
As if it is searching for the fading light.

The metal hook, which used to hold
Baskets of lovingly tended flowers,
Admired by all his friends who came to call,
Now sits accusingly empty,
A signpost to the gradual decay inside,
Weeping its red rust down the wall.

He is idling out his epilogue,
The future is indifferent to him.
He won't be here to enjoy the 'will be',
'The now' is the only tense that is real.
He has no heirs, only chance inheritors.
He ignores distant relatives circling like predators.

EMPTY BOX

"Writing about a writer's block is better than not writing at all."
Charles Bukowski

The virginal paper sheet stares back accusingly,
As I struggle to let my mind run free,
But there is still no sign of any poetry,
Just a fool imprisoned by his illiteracy.
My good intentions have foundered on the rocks,
There are no chocolates left inside my box.

My tortured head a cold and barren void,
Empty of ideas, all thought destroyed,
All usual subterfuges have been deployed,
But my pen remains dry and unemployed.
There are no hands on any of my clocks,
There are no chocolates left inside my box.

How long can I languish here all alone,
Among discarded ideas I've outgrown,
And all those dead poems that I own,
Ignoring all the lifelines I've been thrown ?
There are no keys left to fit any of my locks,
There are no chocolates left inside my box.

I only ask for creativity to be restored,
Not fame or a venal hypocrites reward.
I set sail with so many ideas to be explored,
But that ship has no survivors left on board.
There are no hostages imprisoned in my stocks,
No ships are floating in my docks,
No birds fly in to join my flocks,
I wait but that idea never knocks.
There are no chocolates left inside the box.

TIME

"I'd trade all my tomorrows for one single yesterday."
— *Kris Kristofferson*

The broad shadows of shaded clouds move across
The sodden carpet of translucent, half rotted leaves,
Autumn has spread across my pathway, reminding me
How the seasons remorselessly steal my time, like thieves.

Time runs past me like a river, unfathomable, unstoppable,
Flowing towards some unknown destination in the future.
I reach out to hold it back, it slips through my fingers,
Yet one more moment I have lost and can never recapture.

Only poets, and condemned prisoners on death row,
Look time directly in its uncompromising face,
To see each unrepeatable minute as it passes,
Valuing every tick of life they can never replace.

I sit, comfortable inside my wrinkles, not seeking admiration,
Yet not looking in a mirror without tasting disappointment.
I know that whatever I desire, the future will not be refused.
How lucky my cat is to live all of her life in the present.

They say that you bring your future with you,
Preordained by actions you have taken in the past.
I would have taken more interest in the present
If I'd known today became a memory quite this fast.

Philosophers say life can only be understood
By looking backwards across the landscape of your life.
What use is such understanding, when irreversible time
Provides no opportunity to wield a corrective knife ?

How many wrongs put right and broken fences mended ?
How many endings found for long forgotten lines ?
How many apologies would never have been needed ?
If I could have only found a way to turn back time.

SCHOOL REUNION

"The consequences of acquiring knowledge are often incalculable and seldom beneficial."   Edward Hyams

There we all were, assembled in the hall,
Like we did at school assembly 50 years before.
There for a school reunion of the class of fifty two,
We were, at best, an undistinguished crew.
Some were there just to have a bit of fun;
Others to show us just how well they'd done;
Some came old long lost friendships to renew;
Others because they just had nothing else to do.

I looked around at all the haggard faces,
And couldn't fit any into their classroom places.
Everyone just looked so old, how could this be ?
Then I remembered, they were all as old as me.
We had all changed since the days of our youth
And were unrecognizable, that was the truth,
So to avoid any embarrassment and shame,
We were given badges on which to write our name.

Jones, who lisped his way through elementary French,
Was now a grey haired magistrate on the local bench.
Brown, sent home for wearing yellow socks,
Was a vicar at St Jude's, consoling errant flocks.
Ex head girl Joan looking just a bit too merry,
After over indulging on the introductory sherry.
Julie, who for boyfriends, could have had her pick,
Now a spinster nurse caring for the sick.

Roger, who won the outstanding sportsman shield,
In a wheelchair following an injury on the rugby field.
Dave the class joker, who knew many a rude recitation,
Had become a boring accountant with no conversation.
June who was the school's prettiest girl by a mile,
Now a small, rotund old lady but with the same flirty smile.
And sexy Sarah Skuse, who had quite a reputation,
Had made marrying rich men a profitable vocation.

I renewed some old friendships, and reminisced
About what we'd done in the years we'd missed.
Promised to stay in touch, and addresses exchanged
Knowing future meetings would not be arranged.
We had little in common, apart from our education,
Which was simply determined by our childhood location.
Few people, allowing for expected exaggeration,
Had been very successful in their chosen occupation.
They had settled for security, because they had to pay
For mortgages, children and foreign holidays.

Then a list of fifteen names were read
Of classmates who were already dead.
Nearly twenty percent of the total class
Had not lived to see this reunion pass.
For all of our privileged education
It did not seem that our generation
Had left our world a much better place,
Or left any lasting mark upon its face.

Apart from teenagers, drugs and rock and roll
We'd provided little food for the nation's soul.
Most of our childhood dreams and expectations
Had been lost in life's day to day frustrations.
Although we'd not achieved much, I confess,
We thought surviving fifty years sufficient success.
Despite everything, there was a sense we'd paid our due
Amongst most of the class of fifty two.

So when we left and went our separate ways,
Having failed to recapture past schooldays,
That road we'd walked down, full of hope in our teens,
Was now just a sad boulevard of all our broken dreams.

ANSWERS

"The trouble with life isn't that there is no answer,
it's that there are so many answers." Ruth Benedict

You are asking me for answers
But I have none to give.
I cannot tell you how you'll die,
I cannot tell you how to live.

I can't see behind closed curtains,
Or what the future has in store,
I can only say you are my son,
No one will ever love you more.

It's time for you to prove to me
That you've got what it takes,
Taking courage from my victories,
And learning from my mistakes.

I am casting you adrift today,
To sail out on your own,
To go wherever the winds take you
Using the map that you've been shown.

You will take your memories with you
Hold them safely in your heart,
They will guide you into harbour
As well as any coastal chart.

Now you are the captain,
Because I've given you command,
You'll chose the crew to travel with
They'll be the ones with whom you'll stand.

When you're in the heat of battle
Surrounded by the enemy,
Make sure you're standing by a friend
Now you cannot stand by me.

If you're wounded and you're hurting
Find a woman whose fingers are kind,
Go to her for healing and comfort,
Any calls to me will be declined.

Don't ask me how you'll find true love,
Because how am I to know ?
I found true love by accident
And it was a long, long time ago.

True love cannot be ordered,
True love cannot be bought,
It will come when least expected
If you are ready to be caught.

Avoid those who make false promises,
And those who flatter to deceive,
Remember what you give to others
Determines what you will receive.

I know sometime in the future,
Having found your answers on the way,
You will tell your own son everything
That I'm telling you today.

I have given you everything I could
To prepare you for what's ahead,
But I won't be with you on your travels,
I can't be with you when I'm dead.

I hope you do discover paradise,
I hope you do find true happiness,
But don't come searching for me son,
Because I won't be at this address.

GET USED TO IT

*"You have to accept the fact that sometimes you are the pigeon
and sometimes you are the statue."*   Claude Chabrol

Your party invites are rare to the point of extinction,
You are not part of the in-crowd social set,
You live alone, like an exile in suburbia,
A choirboy in a barbershop quartet.
You feel that no one around understands you,
Your face just never seems to fit,
Don't think you are the only one,
Life's not meant to be easy, just get used to it.

The queue you are in is always the slowest,
The line of cars you join comes to a halt,
Traffic lights change to red as you approach,
Change for the meter is ten pence short.
That expensive watch you've just purchased,
Has since proved to be counterfeit.
Don't think the world is against you,
Life's not meant to be easy, just get used to it.

You can't find the end of the Sellotape,
Or remember that password which you changed,
That bargain on-line purchase is lost in the post,
Your doctor's appointment has been rearranged.
Your computer freezes for no reason,
Your urgent text message fails to transmit,
Modern life is full of these frustrations,
Life's not meant to be easy, just get used to it.

You hurt in all the places where you used to have fun,
Things you used to remember you now forget,
Your life is empty but filling up with time,
There are so many things you've done that you regret.
Your ears full of silence, your eyes full of tears,
You just wish that once more you could be fit.
It's called getting old and can't be avoided,
Life's not meant to be easy, just get on with it.

OLD FRIENDS

"I get by with a little help from my friends." Lennon

An old friend will offer understanding,
When even they don't understand,
Regardless of when, or in what place,
Theirs will be the helping hand.
They will give you shelter from the storm,
They will keep your defences manned.
You'll find safety within the bonds of friendship.

Old friends can see inside your soul,
They know what you have seen,
They will catch you when you trip and fall,
They will laugh at what might have been.
When you make mistakes, they'll forgive you,
Theirs the shoulders on which you lean.
There is no blame inside the bonds of friendship.

If you are falling into the darkness,
Old friends will lift you into the light.
Friends won't question you or doubt you,
Just make sure you're ready for the fight.
They won't criticise or censure you,
But just sympathise with your plight.
There are no critics inside the bonds of friendship.

New friends aren't anchored in your history,
They'll blow away in a hostile wind,
But old friends will still be with you
Whether you've succeeded or you've sinned.
They will not judge you or condemn you,
When all your hopes on them are pinned.
There are no judges inside the bonds of friendship.

Now I have seen what life has to offer
I tell you of all the things that I have done,
The most important are the friendships made,
Not the riches gained or the battles won,
Those long friendships that existed
Before my search for fortune had begun.
True riches are found within the bonds of friendship

WHAT HAVE THEY DONE WITH FUN

"Do not take life too seriously. You will never get out of it alive."
Elbert Hubbard

What have they done with fun?
Where has all the fun gone?
Has it all been outsourced to Canton?
Is it in the library at the Sorbonne?
Does anyone know what they've done?

What have they done with fun ?
Have they sold it all off to the toffs,
Who'll waste it watching plays by Chekov,
And listening to Rachmaninov ?
Is that where all the fun's gone ?

What have they done with fun ?
Why is everything so serious ?
Now you cannot be spontaneous,
Everything is unhealthy or dangerous,
They have put an embargo on fun.

What have they done with fun ?
Has it been killed by health and safety rules ?
Banning skipping and conkers at schools,
Telling us snowballing's only for fools,
And it's dangerous to play in the sun.

What have they done with fun ?
Is it only available by subscription ?
Or provided on a doctor's prescription ?
Is it banned under some court's jurisdiction ?
Tell me can anything be done ?

What have they done with fun ?
Please tell me where it can be found,
There must still be some of it around,
Or was it all lost on the battleground
When the war against innocence was won.
.

What have they done with fun ?
Has it simply just withered and died ?
Despite how hard some of us tried,
The killjoys would not be denied.
Has my generation finally killed off fun ?

VALIDATION VILLANELLE

"In addition to water, air, earth and fire, there is a fifth element essential for life: its name is poetry."   Corina Abdulahm-Negura

Poets exist through the poems they create,
And by means of their passion and artistry,
Raise the mind to a higher state.

They are tortured endlessly by this debate,
Can creating beauty from others misery,
The life of a poet validate ?

Lovers' desire and despair they will translate,
Using cadence, rhyme and symmetry,
To raise the mind to a higher state.

Will lines showing the affinity of love and hate,
And the creation of romantic imagery,
The life of a poet validate ?

When hoping their souls to liberate,
They find no answers in divinity
To raise the mind to a higher state.

They live hidden truths to illustrate,
Using their verses hidden geometry,
To raise minds to a higher state,
And the life of the poet validate.

,

ARE YOU HAPPY ?

*"The standard rebuke to anyone who claims to be happy
is either that they're selfish or living in denial."* Marty Rubin

Driving home through slanting rain,
A distant shaft of wet sunshine
Drips into my eyes.
Raindrops race diagonally across the windows
Desperate to resume their downward journey.
The green hills are piled up like melons
Beyond the fresh laid, quickthorne hedge.

The rainclouds drift away,
I open the window.
The wind hits against half of my face,
Blowing in my memories
Which I allow to travel through my head.
I have no need for the past, so let them
Fall at my feet for someone else to find.

The person driving has metamorphosed
From child to woman in just one summer,
Wearing an almost too tight sweater
And flesh packed jeans, an avalanche of
Light brown hair tumbles across her shoulders.
She is singing along with the radio,
Her tongue like a small bird, caged in ivory.

She knows I am a wannabe writer.
"Why are all the poems you write so sad ?"
She asks, "Aren't you happy ?
Where do you find all that sadness ?"
Innocent questions, penetrating
Into uncomfortable regions
Of my subconscious.

I am as happy as most, I reply.
I'm a sad clown performing in a
Circus of my own words;
A trader of pre-owned despair;
A dealer in second hand dreams;
A thief of other people's thoughts;
A writer of counterfeit conversations.

Am I happier than others ?
How is it possible to tell when so many
Are just pretending to be happy ?
Happiness anyway is a transitory state.
She has yet to discover her
Happiness will only be measured
Against the depth of her sadness.

I think back to when I was her age
And my optimism was still alive.
I was trying to lose my innocence then,
Not like now, regain it.
Sometime between then and now
I must have lost it,
But I can't remember when or how.

We drive on, racing our shadow,
Beneath a grey blue, postcard perfect sky,
Streaked with high altitude cirrus,
Content within our own dreams.
For a moment I think, if I could steal her
Dreams, I'd use them as my own. But maybe
Being young isn't that good anymore.

We reach my home. Her fingers flutter
A goodbye as she leaves, to pursue
Her own version of happiness,
Me to drink again with others
In the café of lost youth.
Happy or not, there is no place
I'd rather be than in this house.

I pour myself a drink,
Sit down, and start to write.
I feel happy

SILENCE

"Never miss a good chance to shut up."
Will Rogers

Walking along the crowded inner city streets,
I pass faces that have mouthed a million words,
Most of which have been discarded carelessly,
Many of which simply floated away unheard.

How many precious words are wasted every day
On pointless conversations or bored refrains,
After all the work that each one of them required
To prize them from the recess of our brains ?

Each word you employ should be used like a rapier
Aimed, not at the ears, but straight at the heart,
Remembering each word unsheathed may be lethal,
And every word that you use, leaves a mark.

Never use words just to drown out a silence,
Leaving them lost like drops of rain in the sea,
Only use them when you have a target to aim at,
Only then, should you set your words free.

Silence is the pearl in an ocean of noise,
Capture and cherish it whenever it's found,
Some of the most beautiful words ever written
Were first heard in the total absence of sound.

Don't rush past a silence, wrap it tightly round you
Let it caress your skin and enter every pore,
Its vocabulary is better than that of any poet
Speaking a truth that you should never ignore.

Only the old are happy to sit alone in silence,
An action rejected by today's impatient youth,
Who search for meaning in celebrity sound-bites,
While the old are already in possession of the truth.

Maybe all these words I use here have been wasted,
And they would have been better withheld in my mind,
I should have written you three minutes of silence
Leaving the substance of this verse undefined.

LOSS

SCARBOROUGH STEPS
For Lorraine 2016

She lives beneath the crying sky, pressed up against a foam-
flecked sea,
In a clifftop house, hugged close by rhododendrons, her clock
ticks away our time.
She offers you shelter from the approaching storm
Then, when the sun sneaks through the window,
She will walk you through the stained glass dappled hall,
To take you on a scenic cliff top ride,
And watch the evening ocean tide,
As she holds you tightly to her side,
While talking of life and suicide,
And other truths of which we rarely speak.

She takes you to a church, set on a rain veiled cobbled road,
Where Rossetti clothed the stones with his romantic artistry,
Where she tells you of those Pre-Raphaelites,
Their lovers and their brotherhood.
Then leaving, with downward steps onto the shore,
She serves you cake and cinnamon tea,
While the gulls shriek out their misery,
And a rainbow surrenders to the sea,
While she talks of death and poetry,
And other truths of which we rarely speak.

We drove through wooded hills, clad in their autumn leaves,
Painted the colour of molten lava by the late October sun.
The tortuous path of the country road hid its ending,
Like a metaphor for the enigma of our own lives.
Cocooned inside the car we become philosophical.
Did big bang or God the universe create ?
Have we at any time outwitted fate ?
Have we souls death will liberate ?
Does love all actions validate ?
And other truths of which we rarely speak.

She is asking me the question, "What is life really for ?
When we have no god to satisfy, is love the only answer ?"
But I can find no words. My lips are sealed
By the poverty of my own wisdom.
There is little time left to answer this question.
We are near the edge, we are in the queue,
There is nothing she or I can do,
But hold on tight and see it through,
Until the end comes into view,
When all the truths we spoke of are revealed.

After Lorraine December 2018

But now I walk alone down the tree shadowed, shoreline paths,
Looking up to that distant clifftop house that was her home.
I hear her laughter on the wind, which steals through the leaves,
Creating dancing points of sunlight on my shoes.
The only one who understood the question has gone.
I have just my thoughts for company,
Still held hostage in life's custody,
While she has reached her epiphany,
Liberated in death she's been set free,
To be the first of us to discover that elusive truth.

We too will make that journey, which everyone must take alone,
The highpoints of our life, scraped flat by the roller of time,
Yesterday's trivia washed away by a greater anguish.
Time's thief stole life from her, and will from everyone,
The world without her is a colder, less joyful place.
We are all diminished by her defeat,
She showed life can be lived without deceit,
That beauty exists where truth and goodness meet,
The beauty that she carried without conceit.
Maybe, when we all find the truth, we will find that beauty too.

THEN THERE WAS ONE

"What have I become my sweetest friend ?
Everyone I know goes away in the end."
Trent Reznor

Those vibrant flowers cut with selfish indifference,
This morning, are now limp corpses dying one by one.
I caused their death, I didn't give them any warning,
Now I wish I could undo what I have done.

We too cannot predict the time of our last breath,
Some malevolent, unknown hand controls our destiny,
Deciding which one of us will be the first to die,
And is as casual about taking life as me.

One by one my old friends have departed,
And I am left here stranded, by cruel circumstance,
On an isle between enlightenment and certain death,
Truth and reality only separated by my ignorance.

My world has contracted with each fallen, fellow partisan,
My optimism wounded by each arrow of distress,
I am left here abandoned, feigning indifference,
Wearing laughter, like armour, against my loneliness.

All those old friends who walked with me so far,
With whom I shared both failure and success,
They could have warned me of their impending exit,
I would not have loved them any less.

Their names are all still there on my telephone,
I just can't bring myself to press delete,
That would make it all seem too permanent,
It would mark too clearly the point of their defeat.

Now their voices and faces are difficult to recall,
My memories of them are fading fast,
Disintegrating as I reach out for them,
Darkness descending like an eyelid on my past.

Life has stopped giving and is now taking away,
But I am not searching for any substitute embrace,
No matter my voice no longer demands attention,
When I am gone, silence will soon fill my place.

I have no fear of the approaching darkness,
Or the finality of the all-consuming flames,
When some unknown, uncomprehending hand,
Will add me to the list of all their names.

I am moving inexorably towards the exit,
If you think of me less often, I will not mind,
I leave behind me nothing but apologies,
And these inadequate, few ephemeral lines.

THE FUNERAL OF A NICE MAN

"To avoid criticism, do nothing, say nothing, and be nothing."
Elbert Hubbard

The low, rust red brick buildings
Crouched down into the grass, as if
Apologizing for the melancholic nature of their application.
The car park filled up fast.
A noiseless black hearse crept in last.
I was not there from choice but to fulfill my sense of obligation.

The participants in this ceremony
Were born in the same village,
Ten green country miles to the west, over seventy years ago.
They stood holding a folded card,
On which the dead man's smiling image
Looked back at them, as if daring them to let him go.

We sat close together.
They were playing the theme
From Last of the Summer Wine as we shuffled in. It was full.
The droning eulogy and speeches
Were shorter than they seemed,
But, from what was audible, the dead man's life seemed dull.

This man, who lay there silently,
Clad in polished golden oak,
Had lost that fight that none of us can ever hope to win.
A kind and gentle man,
According to all those who spoke,
For whom forgiveness was not needed as he never aspired to sin.

I sat, half listening, as his relatives
Recounted his uneventful life.
The congregation smiled dutifully at a well-rehearsed bon mot.
The only ones visibly grieving
Were his daughter and his wife,
As for myself, I felt no grief, our friendship was too long ago.

He had done nothing for the world
To record or remember,
Just his wife and his child will mark where he has been,
And I got to thinking,
On that cold day in September,
If the funerals of the rest of us I had now foreseen.

Did this group, all clad in somber
Shades of black and gray,
Come to celebrate the life just ended, or to commiserate
With his widow? They had been thinking
All week of what to say,
Deciding only he was good at football and he was never late.

These people reluctantly
Assembled there to mourn,
Had not moved far, except for the occasional Spanish holiday,
Still living close to the place
Where they were born.
They had never seen any reason why they should move away.

The careworn, life scored,
Faces reflected their anxiety,
Not about the uncertainty and inhumanity of world events,
But more likely from concerns
Of their children's impropriety,
And how the young are all so devoid of common sense.

Wars in far-flung, foreign places
With hundreds dead,
Places they could not even point to on the global map,
Were not reported in the
Local papers, that they read,
Which devoted one full column to this one dead chap.

The rain heavy, gunmetal grey sky
Reflected our mood,
As we were unavoidably confronted by our own mortality.
It was lifted by the arrival of urns of tea
And post service food,
Helping time separated friends escape the funereal formality.

Once we had shaken hands,
Kissed cheeks and reminisced,
There was little else than childhood memories that we shared.
We spoke weasel words to his widow,
How he would be sadly missed,
But very soon, immersed in self, had forgotten that we cared.

We recalled shared memories
Of childhood escapades,
Roaming the countryside, optimistic and free from fear.
With packed up lunches
And cloudy homemade lemonade,
With no thought then of our present ephemeral tears.

It's much too late now to achieve
All of our youthful ambitions,
All of those brave project plans which came to naught.
No time left for us to win
World-wide fame and recognition,
We will only be remembered in some friend's transient thought.

I was reminded how tenuous my hold
On life had now become.
In my delusion I am younger than those childhood friends I see,
But in reality, I am older and
Closer to the end than some.
A tear formed in my eye, not for him already gone, it was for me.

A HEART DIVIDED

"Before you pledge your undying love to someone,
make them promise they won't die."   Robert Brault,

I thought her just another Judas,
Then I heard that she had died,
The priest told me I'd soon forget,
My heart told me he lied.
A heart divided by loves passing,
Where her presence and perfumes,
Still haunt the cheerless spaces
In all those old familiar rooms.

We committed to each other,
Joined in the body and the blood,
Making many solemn promises
That neither of us understood.
A heart divided by loves duplicity,
For which forgiveness was assumed,
Cloistered in the curtained sanctum
Of all those old familiar rooms.

But then we were left standing,
Behind a door neither of us closed,
For reasons no one ever owned,
For many secrets not disclosed.
A heart divided by the passion
That hate and treachery consumes,
Living together like two strangers
In all those old familiar rooms.

Something darker than love joined us,
There was soon nowhere left to hide,
Passion no longer enough to hold her
The bonds of love had been untied.
A heart divided by loves fragility,
Images that memories exhume,
Lit by the cold light of the morning
In all those old familiar rooms.

From a mouth stuffed full of silence
No words escape into my space,
Filled only with my memories
Of her rapidly fading face.
A heart divided by loves solitude,
As I sit there hurting in the gloom,
Regretting how our love leaked away
In all those old familiar rooms.

Although our bodies will decay
Our ghosts may still make their escape,
To dreams at the edge of the morning
That make our heart and body ache.
A heart divided by compassion,
For the lost promise of her womb,
Now her shadow fills my footsteps
In all those old familiar rooms.

ANNIVERSARY

"To live in the hearts we leave behind is not to die."
Thomas Campbell

It's a day I try to ignore, but one I can't avoid,
The day you left me and my life was destroyed.
It's a date that will always be engraved on my mind
The last day of happiness, the last day my sun shined.
I heard a lonely dog bark, my sky became dark,
Rain and tears combined to make my eyes blind.

I remember so clearly the spring day that we met,
Your eyes were moss green, hair a shade of brunette.
I see the swell of your bosom and the sway of your hips,
The smell and feel of your skin and the taste of your lips.
I see the tilt of your head, hear the things that you said,
You were the sails on my ships and the drug for my trips.

The day we married was a day I could never forget,
You took me without reservation, said there'd be no regret.
Said your love was forever, it was constant and pure,
You'd not let me go, your love could not be cured.
You promised never to leave me, to hurt or deceive me,
We were both so very sure that our love would endure.

You left me without warning, you didn't play by the rules,
Love is not for the faint hearted, love is only for fools.
The rain dropped onto my lips, but my mouth was dry,
I swallowed all of the sadness that fell from the sky.
Love can tear you apart, love can break open your heart.
With love there isn't a rule that they can teach you in school.

I hope you've found happiness, wherever it is that you are,
You know my love goes with you, you'll be my lucky star.
We're not the first to have loved and lost, many go before,
But an avalanche of sadness has me pinned to the floor.
Everywhere I see your face, nothing else can fill your space,
I stare at the door where the dress still hangs you once wore.

So why did you leave me here ? Why did you go away ?
I find no comfort in others embraces, or in what they say.
Not every anniversary is happy, some make you cry,
Reviving memories which prompt the question why ?
I know when truth is laid bare life's not impartial or fair,
And our mortality would imply,

one of us would be the first to die.

CASPER

"The best thing about love is the trust, the best thing about trust is honesty, and the best thing about honesty is faithfulness."
Anurag Prakash Ray

I lost a friend today
  I miss his friendly face,
    Where he always used to sit
      There's now just an empty space.

I lost a friend today
  I always knew that he'd be there,
    When I felt alone and cold
      He always had some love to share.

I lost a friend today
  Although I knew this day would dawn,
    That didn't ease the hurt I feel
      Now that he has gone.

He gave me everything he had
  But in the end he went away,
    I will miss him being close to me,
      Yes, my old cat died today.

VICTIMS

"Man's inhumanity to man makes countless thousands mourn."
Robert Burns

I looked upon the scene unfolding
Which filled me with a deep foreboding.
The fetid swamp is swathed in mist,
In which large serpents turn and twist,
Through the slime and grey green moss
Emerged a gigantic wooden cross.
Around the cross, in ordered spaces,
Stood winged creatures with spectral faces.
One held out its arms in supplication,
Like an angel at Christ's transfiguration.

As it drew closer, I could see
Empty sockets where its eyes should be,
And from its mouth blood dripped down,
Staining red its snow white gown.
A serpent its right arm adorns,
And on its head a crown of thorns.
Although I was engulfed by fear
I could not move as it drew near.
I tried hard my terror to disguise
As I stared into its sightless eyes.

It spoke no words but its head inclined
And words were forming in my mind.
'You have been chosen and brought to this place,
To answer for the sins of the human race.
We here have suffered grief and pain
For actions carried out in your name.
You will listen to our accusations
And to your victim's condemnations.
Then the creatures came forward one by one
To tell me of the things I'd done.

"I was a victim of your war.
You sent the smart bomb to my door,
Exploding without warning, killing me,
My mother and my family.
You dined with friends as they blew out my brains,
You drank a fine claret as my blood filled the drains.
I am looking forward to your agony
As payment for your tyranny."

"I was a victim of your pollution.
I died slowly waiting for your solution.
Profits have to be made, we were told,
The price I paid will be not getting old.
You sat on your yacht while I breathed in your dust,
Your conscience was clear, in your scientists you trust.
I am looking forward to your death
And the hollow rattle of your last breath."

"I was a victim of your racist abuse,
Dying in the sun at the end of a noose.
You said I'd be safe, that was the law,
All men are equal, that's why we fought the war.
You sat in the chamber where these laws were made
But enforcement was left to the men that you paid.
I am looking forward to your execution,
I have waited too long for retribution."

"I was a victim of rape and lust,
By your army sent to rescue the just.
I am just one of many this happened to,
You say tough, that's just what soldiers do.
You knew but abandoned me to my pain,
Saying they let me live so I shouldn't complain.
I am looking forward to hear you cry,
To your god, for him to let you die."

"I was a victim of your gluttony
You left me to die in agony.
I starved beneath the Somalian sky
It took me thirteen years to die.
But you gave your conscience absolution
With a few pounds charity contribution.
I am looking forward to your suffering
And to watch you slowly perishing."

"I am a victim of your greed,
Taking what you want not what you need.
I worked in your factory fourteen hours a day,
For less than one whole dollars pay.
On the back of my work and poverty,
You lived a life of obscene luxury.
I look forward to your pleas for clemency,
I'll show the same compassion that you showed me."

The sky turned from indigo to black,
I saw the lightening flash, heard the thunder crack.
Suddenly a laser shaft of light
Lit up the cross and its acolytes.
And then a golden child appears,
Above the cross, weeping bloodstained tears.
"I'm crying for humankind," it said,
As golden vultures circled round its head.

.

"I gave you love and honesty
You repaid me with hate and duplicity.
I gave you many chances for redemption
You ignored them all without exception.
Your love of celebrity and self,
Your obsession with creating wealth,
Blinded you to virtue and morality
You are now face to face with your mortality."

"You have heard your victims' condemnation
They are here to exact retaliation.
You must have known, come judgement day,
Someone was going to have to pay.
There will be no pleas or benediction,
They are here to see your crucifixion."
With that the faceless creatures came,
Surrounding me, chanting my name.

The golden vultures all flew in,
Ripping off my clothes and tearing at my skin.
And then my naked bloodstained form,
Spread-eagled in a cruciform,
Was forced against the cross's wooden rails,
In one creature's hand were golden nails,
There was no doubt these nails would fix,
My bleeding body to the crucifix.

The hammer fell, the nails drove in,
Smashing through my bone and skin.
The creatures melted back into the air
Leaving me just hanging there,
Reflecting on those we promised to protect,
Who perished due to our neglect.
I was alone, without my God, without a friend,
Realising this is how my life would end.

A NOTE TO MY EXECUTORS

"Nothing of real worth can ever be bought. Love, friendship, honour, valour, respect. All these things have to be earned." David Gemmell,

When I can no longer marvel at the work of art that is the rose,
Or smell its incense, in air full of the gossamer wings of bees;
No more enjoy the luminous flowers of the clematis, that
Paints itself among the contorted branches of a long dead tree;
When lost to me forever is the hungry blackbird's shrill delight,
As it defeats my elaborate defences,
Guarding bushes laden with jewelled fruit;
Take my place on the seat, where I once paused to reflect,
All I ask is that you treat my garden with respect.

When my effects are distributed to new owners, as yet unknown,
Those precious and sentimental artifacts that enriched my life.
Miniature paintings, scattered like precious jewels on my walls;
My furniture, fashioned in golden oak, by forgotten artisans;
Objects containing nostalgic memories, the signposts of my life.
Such personal possessions, and these few lines,
Are all that I will leave.
I have hidden a fraction of my soul in every item you select,
Please handle them with care and treat them with respect.

When I start my journey to oblivion, or an unexpected heaven,
You may read these inelegant verses and be reminded of my life.
The time has come when I have had to drop the part I played,
My true self emerging from life's deceptions and subterfuge.
My supposed intellect, looted from the waves of late night radio,
Exposed as a shallow camouflage
For the ignorance of a common man.
I hope that you will say, at least as far as you can recollect,
'He always treated his friends with generosity and respect.'

When I am gone scatter me beneath the trees in Owlet Wood,
On emerald moss, lying like green snow drifts on the ground,
Lit by shards of light filtering through tiers of crimpled leaves.
The moss masks your footfall, leaving no memory you've passed,
And the silence flows back into the space you have borrowed.
Do not pollute this place with words,
Nature's silence is the ultimate poetry.
Leave me in that quiet fragile place where nature is unchecked,
All I ask of you is that you treat my memory with respect.

GUILT

No amount of guilt can change the past, and no amount of worrying can change the future."   *Umar Ibn Al-Khattaab*

He is watching television ...
Laughing.
She is in the next room ...
Dying.

He hesitates. He is feeling guilty.
He goes to her, she is sleeping,
Unknowingly one hour
Closer to the end.

He has to leave.
The car is quiet, powerful.
He is travelling east.
The music is soothing.
It is a sunny day.
The autumn colours like
A landscape painting.

Deaths gravity recedes with distance.
He finds himself praying,
In spite of his disbelief.

The guilt endures.

DECISIONS

With Rosi in Edinburgh, June 2002

In life there are many choices to be made,
Which promises to keep, which ones to break,
But none of them can prepare you for,
The one when life itself is what's at stake.

We try to make everything look normal
To those looking at us from outside.
They don't see the turmoil inside our heads,
Or know how often we have cried.

There is no map for the pilgrimage we're on,
But you know you won't be travelling alone,
My arms will be wrapped tightly round you,
They will carry you safely back to home.

I want my love to be your shelter,
When you are battling through the storm,
When icy winds of doubt come to chill you,
I will always keep you safe and warm.

I want my love to be your lifeboat,
When you are crossing waters rough and wide,
When jagged rocks of pain try to sink you,
I will always be there at your side.

I want to take all of your fears away,
And hide them from you in my head,
In return giving you all the strength I have,
For you to use instead.

I have never claimed to be your hero,
I never promised you that I'd be brave,
But you know I'd exchange my life for yours
If only one of us could be saved.

Maybe I can't be the one to save you,
Or to give you back your youth,
But I can hold you close and comfort you,
By sharing your knowledge of the truth.

What more can we do, what more to say,
On this journey without destination boards ?
None of us know how, or when, we'll reach the end
And if oblivion or eternity is our reward.

IT'S TERMINAL

"Brookholme" Scarborough 2016

The consultant said it was terminal,
There was no more they could do.
A full life sentence with no chance of reprieve.
They say she's brave but that's not so,
Acceptance of the inevitable
Is not the stuff of which heroines are made.
She cries alone, so they won't see that she's afraid.

The rays of the rising sun
Illuminate the paintings on her wall.
She tries to imprint the image on her mind
In case there comes a time when she can't see.
She has woken early as usual,
The unfailing alarm clock of pain,
Interrupting her fitful sleep again.

She looks out of the window, towards the sea,
Where paper white, cut out gulls,
Drift against the sky's blue lacquered screen.
If she had her brother's artist hands,
She would transfer this transient scene,
Of the new laid colour of morning's transition,
Into a more permanent composition.

The birds have risen before her
And cling, like feathered acrobats,
Onto their hanging, caged nut, feast.
An ink stain crow appears, the small birds flee.
When her carefully planned defences defeat it,
The crow abandons its attempt to steal,
And the finches return to their topsy-turvy meal.

She gazes down into the garden where
The algae covered, fern fringed pond,
Awaits the annual invasion of amorous frogs.
The buds are forming on the roses, enclosing
Vermillion petals within their hidden heart.
The sound of the sea stealing into her ears,
And her garden, help to put a lid on her fears.
.

She looks at her collection of assorted antiques,
Collected when life was carefree and fun,
At all the books, paintings and perfumes,
Each one owning a small part of her life.
Now they are but cruel reminders,
These old artefacts from the past,
That few of life's pleasures will last.

Standing again at the window looking out to sea,
One over eager tree impinges on her view,
Its impertinence annoys her.
Thin streaks of foam marble the waves
And a large ship floats uncaring across the horizon.
She has always loved the view from these windows
And will take it with her no matter where she goes.

Flying columns of rag tag clouds sweep in from the west
To spoil the morning. They weep for her,
Their tears bouncing, like shards of glass,
Off of the Rhododendron leaves.
She turns away. She has another day to live,
Balanced precariously between her pain
And morphine's sly subversion of her brain.

MORPHINE

"To die will be an awfully big adventure."
J.M. Barrie

Come on death, come and get me, I think I've had enough.
There's nothing else to take from me, you've already taken love.
I'm not looking for the secret of survival,
I no longer need to pretend,
I'm not worried about your arrival
Now I have morphine as my friend.

Come on death, don't keep me waiting, you can take me anytime,
Show your face, stop prevaricating, you are often on my mind.
There is no one now who needs me,
There's no one left to defend,
I'm just saying come on and get me
Now I have morphine as my friend.

Come on death, I'm in your sites, I can't escape your hand,
I know that you're within your rights, I promise I understand.
I'm not hiding, cowering in my bed,
That's not the message I want to send,
I'm not curled up in fear and dread,
Now I have morphine as my friend.

Come on death, just do your worst, you don't scare me now,
If I'm the first one on your list I'll be ready anyhow.
You see I'm no longer frightened,
I know you'll get me in the end,
But I'm so much more enlightened
Now I have morphine as my friend.

Come on death, you're less frightening now that I am old,
I know you're closing in on me because I'm feeling cold,
I think I'm ready to give up the fight,
I know you'll nurse me to the end,
I know you'll help me through the night,
Morphine, you are my assassin and my friend.

BUCKET LISTS ARE FUTILE

"Should is a futile word. It's about what didn't happen."
Margaret Atwood

I don't see any point in writing down
A list of things you'd like to see and do.
If you haven't done those things by now
Probably you're never likely too.

I have sampled the icy wastes of Alaska,
Held geisha parties with the Japanese,
Crossed the Golden Gate to the giant redwoods,
Driven the Big Sur to Los Angeles.
I have been halfway up the Amazon,
Watched the sun set red on the Taj Mahal,
Walked the beach on Copacabana,
Listened to Janis Joplin at the Albert Hall.
I have looked out on many golden beaches,
From the inside of many foreign bars,
I have eaten in many a fancy restaurant,
And driven my share of fast, exotic cars.

None compare to one night in a lovers arms,
Or the love of your family and friends,
So before listing out all of your fantasies
This thought to you, I would commend.

Just make a list of all those you love,
With their addresses noted, place by place,
Then alongside them, the date by when,
You'll tell them you love them, face to face.

This is the only list you need to write
Of things you want to do your life to verify.
Don't waste your time on futile fantasies,
They'll be of no value to you when you die.

Me, I've nothing I want to put on my bucket list,
But to let me die a quiet, pain free death,
And one day just be taken by surprise
By the unexpected arrival of that last breath.

EVERYONE WILL DIE ALONE

"Ring down the curtain, the farce is over." Francois Rabelais

The warmonger and the pacifist,
Soldiers in the battle zone,
The coward and the terrorist,
Mother Theresa and Al Capone.
The aesthete and the artist,
The jazzman with his saxophone,
The engineer and the scientist,
Everyone will die alone.

All the losers and all the winners,
The anonymous or the well-known,
All of the Bishops and the sinners,
The king sitting on his thrown,
The banker and the millionaire,
Dictators with images cast in stone,
The pauper with nothing to declare,
Everyone will die alone.

Those with a god to help them,
The atheist with no creed to own,
Those who praise, those who condemn,
The old and others not yet grown.
No matter how many friends you have
They cannot get your end postponed,
Even if you're surrounded by those you love,
All of you will die alone.

EVERYONE WILL DIE ALONE / 2

"Maybe all one can do is hope to end up with the right regrets."
Arthur Miller

Everyone dies alone.
Believers, atheists, saints, sinners, the beggar with
Nothing, the rich man with nothing left to own,
Winners or losers, no one will win this time.
Those with many friends, those with none,
Kings, princes and paupers, are all
The same to Father Death, the
Sole shadowy spectator to
Our last performance.
A stranger will thumb
Closed our eyes.
All of us
Will die
Alone.

LEAVING

"When the people whom we love the most leave us,
we start learning to live with the shadows they have left inside us."
Akshay Vasu

She planned her own leaving with an elysian cortege,
Arranging when to meet them and secretly depart.
They came to her silently while you were sleeping,
And stole her past the guardians of your heart.

There is nothing you can do now to keep her,
She is leaving you by her own command,
She is carried on the shoulders of her lovers
Between the ranks of the favoured and the damned.

She is surrounded by many others on her journey,
Your love affair was never meant to end like this,
Her once full red lips now feel as cold as marble
When you bow to give her one last goodbye kiss.

She has left with her companions in procession,
She is lifted high before seeking lower ground,
Although her leaving was never one you planned for,
You'll always know in future where she can be found.

Her silence is now deep and overwhelming,
Filling the spaces where her laughter used to ring,
She had no final words to say to you on leaving,
She will not thank you for the flowers that you bring.

Where once she would have offered you her passion,
In those cold dark hallways where you stole a kiss,
Now you can find no form of consolation
The time of her leaving was in someone else's gift.

There is no shame in the tears that you are bleeding,
No dishonour in the anger aimed at her Lord,
You carry no blame for the manner of her leaving,
Through the pain your own honour is restored.

Tonight her glass remains untouched on the table,
The bread and wine will not now be consumed,
Tonight there will be no signs of celebration,
Any thoughts of resurrection already doomed.

Now you know it's not a nightmare you are dreaming,
You won't awake and find her sleeping at your side,
You will only waltz her in the ballroom of remembrance,
It's what happens when love and mortality collide.

OWLET WOOD

The evening sunlight filters through
The trees in Owlet Wood,
As if uncertain if it should,
Illuminate the blue Monkshood
Beneath the canopies of oak and yew.

The freshly fallen autumn leaves
Lie loosely on the ground,
In multi-coloured brown,
Like the earth's designer gown,
In a pattern only nature could conceive.

The brambles that are screening
Fallen branches, that lie across
Soft mounds of creeping moss,
Which dome head mushrooms emboss,
Enhance my life and give it meaning.

The eternal, emerald evergreen,
Unlike the brazen deciduous tree,
Never sheds its modesty.
I let its tranquillity envelope me,
Listening to the song of birds I've never seen.

From the branches of a Sycamore tree
Hang children's shoes, stained with dirt,
A straw hat and a football shirt,
All sad reminders of someone's hurt.
The tree holds them close beneath its canopy.

When I feel lonely and downcast
Owlet wood welcomes me in.
Its peace envelopes me like skin,
Its beauty better than any medicine,
Heals the wounds inflicted by my past.

In the silence I can hear the thoughts
That are pouring from my mind.
I am going to leave them all behind,
For someone else to find,
Amongst the Celandine and Bishops Wort.

A solitary oak post stands, its plaque declares,
'The area behind this post you see
is dedicated to Rosemary,
because she loved all trees.'
I stop to look, because my heart is there.

"Here it is -- the final page you turn it and walk away"

Andrew Hussie

Printed in Great Britain
by Amazon